A Currency of Hope

A Currency *of* Hope

In D.A., our purpose is threefold:
to stop incurring unsecured debt,
to share our experience with the newcomer,
and to reach out to other debtors.

DEBTORS
ANONYMOUS

Contents

Foreword to the Second Edition xi
Foreword to the First Edition xiv
A Brief History of Debtors Anonymous xvi
The Twelve Steps of Debtors Anonymous xix
The Twelve Traditions of Debtors Anonymous xxi
The Twelve Concepts for D.A. World Service xxiii
The Signposts on the Road to Becoming a Compulsive Debtor xxv
The Tools of Debtors Anonymous xxvii
The Twelve Promises of Debtors Anonymous xxx
Do You Think You Might Be a Compulsive Debtor? xxxii
Getting Started xxxiv

Our Stories

1 Reflections on Two Decades of D.A. Recovery 3
*An old-timer values the spiritual growth that came through
working the D.A. program.*

2 From Desperation to Daily Gratitude 6
Living a one-day-at-a-time D.A. program for more than twenty years.

3 A New Way of Life 11
Disasters brought him to D.A.—and a new life of recovery.

4   **An Underearner Discovers Real Recovery** 15
    "It doesn't matter how much money I earn. I will always be a debtor."

5   **A Twelve-Step Journey out of Debt** 24
    A journey from deep debt to "blessings and opportunities."

6   **Saved by a Power Greater than Myself** 28
    *This member exchanged a career of debting for a loan-free
    college education.*

7   **Building Clarity, Trust, and Joy** 37
    *Driven to D.A. by the secrets hidden from her spouse, she builds
    a relationship of trust and a spirit of service.*

8   **An Unlikely Debtor** 41
    "I'm a compulsive debtor. When I admit that, my life moves forward."

9   **There's a Monster Living inside Me** 46
    *"When I lost my first tooth, the tooth fairy left an I.O.U. under
    my pillow."*

10 **Thank God for a Long, Slow Recovery** 49
    Crises are replaced with unexpected boons as this debtor develops faith.

11 **Less Is More** 59
    *D.A. gives her the tools to face her financial situation honestly
    and responsibly.*

12 **God Is My Business Partner** 63
    A businesswoman finds a working partnership with her Higher Power.

13 **A Focus on the Basics** 67
    *Working the D.A. program pays big dividends toward this
    debtor's recovery.*

14 **A Storybook Credit Card Debtor** 70
    *His mother gave him his first credit card and his first D.A. meeting.
    He did the rest.*

15 Higher Power Is Driving 75
*She wanted somebody else to take care of her. She knew she
couldn't do it herself.*

16 Watching a Fellowship Grow in the U.K. 78
*She learns to detach from her debts and build her faith in a
spiritual D.A. program.*

17 My Surrender to D.A. 84
*This debtor needed a lot of courage to face her creditors.
She found it with the help of her Pressure Relief Group.*

18 An Entrepreneur Finds D.A. and B.D.A. Recovery 87
*"I do the best and feel the happiest when I know in my bones
that my HP is my source."*

19 Surrender and Service 90
On the road to recovery, this debtor passes milestones to true joy.

20 From Chaos to Clarity in Business 95
*This debtor discovers that not incurring new unsecured personal
debt or business debt leads to freedom from old debt.*

21 Debt Was Hazardous to My Health 98
She couldn't imagine life without credit cards.

22 The Escape Artist 107
This debtor created only prisons until he learned to use the D.A. Tools.

23 From Homelessness to Happiness 113
*She finds a new D.A. community to support her in her recovery
from compulsive debting.*

24 From Fruitless to Fulfilled in D.A. and B.D.A. 117
*"Who was I to say that God would not restore me to sanity around
my business and my income?"*

25   Twenty-one Years of Solvency 121
*Working the Steps and staying solvent bring her out of darkness
to discover her real self.*

26   The Good Old Days: A Fond Look Back 124
D.A. was his last resort. It became his first investment.

27   A Onetime Liar and Cheat Finds a New Life 127
From living off others to a fulfilling, prosperous life of honor and dignity.

28   Dependent on Plastic 132
A compulsive shopper breaks out of a family pattern of secrecy.

29   Loving as Money; Money as Love 137
*Money became her measure for love, and finally, her lover. In D.A.
she learned to be present as a businesswoman, mother, and wife.*

30   Recovery in New Hampshire 143
*D.A. was forty miles away, but it helped so much that this debtor
brought it home.*

31   The Gift of Awareness 147
*Though driven into D.A. with negative net worth and a bad car
loan, she found miracles.*

32   "Scarlett" Comes Home to D.A. 151
A drama queen took debting to the limit and found Higher Power.

33   Mario's Story 154
*With the support of the Fellowship, he stayed solvent throughout
his fatal illness.*

34   Caring for Myself 157
*Though his early family experiences taught him shame, he learned
to value himself in D.A.*

35   Financial Fantasy Gives Way to Bright Reality 161
He finds the gift of clarity through the Twelve Steps.

36 **D.A. Recovery: Take Two** 164
A debtor drives to the edge before turning back to D.A.

37 **No Longer a Thief** 169
*This woman stopped taking from others after learning how to
give to herself.*

38 **The Answer to a Family Disease** 174
*She blamed others until she learned to accept her own powerlessness over
compulsive debting.*

How to Find Debtors Anonymous 176

Foreword to the Second Edition

The publication of *A Currency of Hope* was a cherished achievement of historic importance for Debtors Anonymous. Published in early 1999, it provided D.A. members with a focal point of shared experience, pride, and unity, and offered precious hope and the promise of freedom to countless numbers of those suffering from the disease of compulsive debting. It is also a snapshot of the Fellowship of the day. Many of the stories told moving accounts of the recovery that so many of us have experienced when we stopped incurring new, unsecured debt and began a life guided by the Twelve Steps and a commitment to service. But in many other stories, our primary purpose—the desire to stop incurring new unsecured debt and the willingness to reach out to another debtor—is insufficiently stressed.

Since then, the Fellowship has become increasingly focused on the need for Debtors Anonymous to maintain a singleness of purpose in order to make the hope of recovery available to those who still suffer. In her Annual Report to the 2006 World Service Conference in San Diego, the Chair of the General Service Board stressed that the health of the Fellowship, indeed its existence, depended on adhering to our primary purpose. Her statement continues to influence the review and production of literature, both in print and on the website.

In 2008, the World Service Conference approved the concept of collecting a new round of stories from members with strong, long-term recovery. Writers would have not incurred new unsecured debt continuously for at least three years and would have experience with the Debtors Anonymous program of recovery, including the Twelve Steps, the Twelve Traditions, sponsorship, service, and the Tools. The Communications Committee of the General Service Board, which brought the motion, noted that they were doing so to respond to many members' desire "for more clarity on what constitutes strong recovery in Debtors Anonymous."

By the 2009 World Service Conference, fifteen stories had been collected, and that year the Conference approved the concept of posting the ongoing collection of "recovery stories" on the D.A. website. The following year, the Conference approved "the concept of publishing the second edition of *A Currency of Hope*, in which stories . . . recommended for removal be replaced by the Board-approved recovery stories from our D.A. website."

This edition comprises thirty-eight stories of recovery from compulsive debting. Seventeen stories were carried over from the first edition of *A Currency of Hope*; the remaining twenty-one were originally published in *Ways & Means*, the Debtors Anonymous members' newsletter, and the D.A. website. Like its predecessor, this edition is a mirror of the Fellowship. Our members are dedicated to not incurring new, unsecured debt; seeking recovery through the Twelve Steps; and making this singular spiritual solution available to the debtor who still suffers.

Two editorial notes about the language in these stories. Readers will find both the word "solvency" and the word "abstinence"; in Debtors Anonymous, the meaning is identical: not incurring new, unsecured debt. Second, a fundamental principle is expressed in the variety of spiritual experiences that are recounted. By not incurring new, unsecured debt a day at a time, and by undertaking the suggested program of recovery offered by the Twelve Steps, many members have gratefully opened to a belief in a Power greater than themselves, whether they call that larger reality God, a Higher Power, Holy Spirit, or simply sanity.

Debtors Anonymous, like all human endeavors, is a work in progress. In our fourth decade, we are a far more varied Fellowship than ever before and our stories will increasingly reflect this continuing evolution. D.A. is flourishing outside North America: at this writing, there are groups on six continents. Future editions will continue to offer the remarkable journeys of D.A. members, in the unique Twelve Step process of one debtor sharing recovery heart to heart with another.

Foreword to the First Edition

We, the men and women of Debtors Anonymous, come together to solve our common problem of compulsive debting. We share our experience, strength and hope with one another to arrest the disease of debting. We have found compulsive debting to be a painful, confusing and destructive disorder. Compulsive debting takes many forms from incurring unsecured debt to compulsive shopping, from grandiose thinking to deprivation mentality. All these symptoms of debting seriously affect our quality of life—financially, emotionally, mentally, spiritually, physically, and socially.

As members of Debtors Anonymous, we have chosen a spiritual path of healing and growth which requires working the "Twelve Steps" and using the "Twelve Tools of D.A." The Twelve Steps form the foundation for our recovery. The D.A. Tools aid us in working the Steps. As a result of beginning this recovery process, we have been able to stop incurring new unsecured debt, one day at a time, and to retire our existing debt through reasonable debt repayment within our means. We are learning to understand ourselves and form genuine loving connections with others and discover a relationship with a Higher Power of our own choice.

We have created this recovery book to share our Program with other compulsive debtors so that they might understand what we have come to know about debting and experience the relief we have found. The stories we have gathered are a collection of members' experiences with debting which share: "What it was like for them, What happened, How they changed, and What it is like now." These stories express the opinions and experiences of the individual member and not necessarily those of Debtors Anonymous as a whole.

We hope that if you identify with some, or all, aspects of compulsive debting, you will join us on the path of recovery from compulsive debting and find the peace, joy, hope and love that is here for you.

A Brief History of
Debtors Anonymous

The idea that would give rise to the Fellowship of Debtors Anonymous started in 1968, when a core group of recovering members of Alcoholics Anonymous began discussing the problems they were experiencing with money. Led by a man named John H., they began an eight-year spiritual odyssey to understand the causes and conditions behind their self-destructive behavior with money.

Having little idea of how to approach this, they focused in turn on their diverse symptoms, including many different patterns of spending, saving, shopping, and earning. They first called themselves the "Penny Pinchers," and attempted to control through will power the amount of money they spent. Later, the group renamed itself the "Capital Builders," convinced that their financial problems stemmed from an inability to save money. They tried to cure this by making daily deposits into savings accounts, but this, too, failed to resolve their problems.

For the next few years, the ever-changing group of people around John H. tried addressing all of the symptoms they were suffering from, but continued to fail. In addition to A.A., they attended meetings of Gamblers Anonymous, Al-Anon, and other twelve-step fellowships, hoping to find a definitive answer. Finally, as more years passed, they began to understand that their monetary problems did not stem from an inability to save or control the amount they spent or earned, but rather from the inability to stop incurring unsecured debt.

By 1971, the essence of the D.A. Program unfolded in the discovery and understanding that the act of debting itself was the threshold of the disease, and the only solution was to use the Twelve Steps of Alcoholics Anonymous to stop incurring new unsecured debt one day at a time and to help others to do so. After two years, the group of recovering A.A. members disbanded. Meetings came and went, with John H. attempting desperately to hold the small and ever-changing group of financially troubled alcoholics together.

D.A. re-emerged in April 1976 when John H. and another debtor met at St. Stephen's Rectory in New York City for the first regularly scheduled D.A. meeting. Within a year, a second meeting was organized, with members outside of A.A. for the first time. By early 1982, there were five meetings in existence in the world, all of them in Manhattan.

In March 1982, representatives from those five meetings took a daring step. With many of them having been inspired by their service experience in A.A., they established a Pro-Tem Board of Trustees for D.A. The Pro-Tem Board of five scheduled an Annual Meeting of Debtors Anonymous, held in New York City in September 1982. A permanent General Service Board for the Fellowship was created at that meeting, and has existed ever since. Newly established meetings in Boston and Washington D.C. also elected Regional Trustees, and these were later joined by a Regional Trustee from Los Angeles.

D.A. remained mostly New York–based during the mid 1980s, and four more Annual Meetings were held from 1983 to 1986, all in Manhattan. The General Service Board during this era attempted to build a service structure for the fledgling Fellowship largely on the model of A.A., but with some differences to accommodate D.A.'s much smaller size. Class B (non-debtor) trustees were added to the GSB, and the Regional Trustees were replaced by a board composed entirely of trustees to be drawn from throughout the world, in the interests of D.A. unity.

In 1987, the GSB further followed the A.A. model by creating a World Service Conference and turning to it for guidance and direction for D.A.'s future. In a bid to create a truly broad-based Fellowship, the Conference met the first year in New York but in subsequent years in Los Angeles, Boston, Chicago, San Francisco, and many other cities. Today, more than a hundred delegates attend the Conference annually.

The biggest challenges in D.A.'s first fifteen years were the development of a service structure, the writing and adoption of a common literature, the overcoming of regional differences, and the forging of D.A. unity. In 1994, the growing importance of Intergroups was recognized when Intergroup Service Representatives joined General Service Representatives and Trustees as delegates to the annual World Service Conference.

Like most new organizations, D.A. struggled financially in its early years. On several occasions its financial position has been perilous. Initially, volunteers fielded requests for information about D.A. A General Service Office was established in 1985 and was open a few hours a week for many years. D.A.'s original office was located in New York, but moved to the Boston area shortly before its first full-time employee was hired in 2001.

As of publication of the second edition of *A Currency of Hope*, Debtors Anonymous has more than five hundred registered meetings in more than fifteen countries worldwide. D.A. has its own website, two quarterly newsletters (the *DA Focus* and *Ways & Means*), a large stock of recovery pamphlets and service materials including its own Debtors Anonymous Manual for Service, and is engaged in producing translations of D.A. copyrighted materials for D.A. groups around the world.

The Twelve Steps of Debtors Anonymous

1. We admitted we were powerless over debt—that our lives had become unmanageable.

2. Came to believe that a Power greater than ourselves could restore us to sanity.

3. Made a decision to turn our will and our lives over to the care of God as we understood Him.

4. Made a searching and fearless moral inventory of ourselves.

5. Admitted to God, to ourselves, and to another human being the exact nature of our wrongs.

6. Were entirely ready to have God remove all these defects of character.

7. Humbly asked Him to remove our shortcomings.

8. Made a list of all persons we had harmed and became willing to made amends to them all.

9. Made direct amends to such people wherever possible, except when to do so would injure them or others.

10. Continued to take personal inventory and when we were wrong, promptly admitted it.

11. Sought through prayer and meditation to improve our conscious contact with God as we understood Him, praying only for knowledge of His will for us and the power to carry that out.

12. Having had a spiritual awakening as the result of these steps, we tried to carry this message to compulsive debtors, and to practice these principles in all our affairs.

The Twelve Traditions of Debtors Anonymous

1. Our common welfare should come first; personal recovery depends upon D.A. unity.

2. For our group purpose there is but one ultimate authority—a loving God as He may express Himself in our group conscience. Our leaders are but trusted servants; they do not govern.

3. The only requirement for D.A. membership is a desire to stop incurring unsecured debt.

4. Each group should be autonomous except in matters affecting other groups or D.A. as a whole.

5. Each group has but one primary purpose—to carry its message to the debtor who still suffers.

6. A D.A. group ought never endorse, finance, or lend the D.A. name to any related facility or outside enterprise, lest problems of money, property, or prestige divert us from our primary purpose.

7. Every D.A. group ought to be fully self-supporting, declining outside contributions.

XXII | A CURRENCY OF HOPE

8. Debtors Anonymous should remain forever nonprofessional, but our service centers may employ special workers.

9. D.A. as such, ought never be organized; but we may create service boards or committees directly responsible to those they serve.

10. Debtors Anonymous has no opinion on outside issues; hence the D.A. name ought never be drawn into public controversy.

11. Our public relations policy is based on attraction rather than promotion; we need always maintain personal anonymity at the level of press, radio, and films.

12. Anonymity is the spiritual foundation of all our traditions, ever reminding us to place principles before personalities.

The Twelve Concepts for D.A. World Service

Just as the Twelve Steps are guides for personal recovery and the Twelve Traditions are guides for group unity, the Twelve Concepts are guides for World Service. These Concepts serve as a path for Twelfth Step work on a world service level, and show how the D.A. groups, the World Service Conference, and the Debtors Anonymous General Service Board work together to carry recovery in D.A. to the still suffering debtor.

1. The ultimate responsibility and authority for Debtors Anonymous World Services should always remain with the collective conscience of our whole Fellowship as expressed through the D.A. groups.

2. The D.A. groups have delegated complete administrative and operational authority to the General Service Board. The groups have made the Conference the voice and conscience for the whole Fellowship, excepting for any change in the Twelve Steps, Twelve Traditions, and in Article 10, the General Warranties of the Conference Charter.

3. As a traditional means of creating and maintaining a clearly defined working relationship between the groups, the World Service Conference, and the Debtors Anonymous General Service Board, it is suggested that we endow these elements of world service with a traditional "Right of Decision" in order to ensure effective leadership.

4. Throughout our Conference structure, we maintain at all levels a traditional "Right of Participation," ensuring a voting representation.

5. The traditional Rights of Appeal and Petition protect the minority opinion and ensure the consideration of personal grievances.

6. The Conference acknowledges the primary administrative responsibility of the Debtors Anonymous General Service Board.

7. The Conference recognizes that the Charter and the Bylaws of the Debtors Anonymous General Service Board serve as governing documents and that the Trustees have legal rights, while the rights of the Conference are spiritual, rooted in the Twelve Traditions. The Concepts are not legal instruments.

8. The Debtors Anonymous General Service Board of Trustees assumes primary leadership for larger matters of overall policy, finance, and custodial oversight, and delegates authority for routine management of the General Service Office.

9. Good leaders, together with appropriate methods for choosing them at all levels, are necessary. At the world service level, the Board of Trustees assumes primary leadership for D.A. as a whole.

10. Every D.A. service responsibility should be equal to its service authority as defined by tradition, resolution, or D.A.'s Charter.

11. While the Trustees hold final authority for D.A. World Service administration, they will be assisted by the best possible staff members and consultants. Therefore, serious care and consideration will always be given to the compensation, selection, induction to service, rotation, and assignments for special rights and duties for all staff with a proper basis for determining financial compensation.

12. The Conference of Debtors Anonymous will observe the spirit of the Traditions, taking care not to become powerful and wealthy; having sufficient operating funds with a prudent reserve; having no authority over any other members; making important decisions by discussing and voting on issues wherever possible by substantial unanimity; not acting in a punitive way; not inciting public controversy; never performing any acts of government; and finally, always remaining democratic in thought and action.

The Signposts on the Road to Becoming a Compulsive Debtor

1. Being unclear about your financial situation. Not knowing account balances, monthly expenses, loan interest rates, fee, fines, or contractual obligations.

2. Frequently "borrowing" items such as books, pens, or small amounts of money from friends and others, and failing to return them.

3. Poor saving habits. Not planning for taxes, retirement or other nonrecurring but predictable items, and then feeling surprised when they come due; a "live for today, don't worry about tomorrow" attitude.

4. Compulsive shopping: Being unable to pass up a "good deal"; making impulsive purchases; leaving price tags on clothes so they can be returned; not using items you've purchased.

5. Difficulty in meeting basic financial or personal obligations, and/or an inordinate sense of accomplishment when such obligations are met.

6. A different feeling when buying things on credit than when paying cash, a feeling of being in the club, of being accepted, of being grown up.

7. Living in chaos and drama around money: Using one credit card to pay another; bouncing checks; always having a financial crisis to contend with.

8. A tendency to live on the edge: Living paycheck to paycheck; taking risks with health and car insurance coverage; writing checks hoping money will appear to cover them.

9. Unwarranted inhibition and embarrassment in what should be a normal discussion of money.

10. Overworking or underearning: Working extra hours to earn money to pay creditors; using time inefficiently; taking jobs below your skill and education level.

11. An unwillingness to care for and value yourself: Living in self-imposed deprivation; denying your basic needs in order to pay your creditors.

12. A feeling or hope that someone will take care of you if necessary, so that you won't really get into serious financial trouble, that there will always be someone you can turn to.

The Tools of
Debtors Anonymous

Recovery from compulsive debting begins when we stop incurring new, unsecured debt, one day at a time. (Unsecured debt is any debt that is not backed up by some form of collateral, such as a house or other asset.) We attain a daily reprieve from compulsive debting by practicing the Twelve Steps and by using the following tools.

1. **Meetings**
   We attend meetings at which we share our experience, strength, and hope with one another. Unless we give to newcomers what we have received from D.A., we cannot keep it ourselves.

2. **Record Maintenance**
   We maintain records of our daily income and expenses, of our savings, and of the retirement of any portions of our outstanding debts.

3. **Sponsorship**
   We have found it essential to our recovery to have a sponsor and to be a sponsor. A sponsor is a recovering debtor who guides us through the Twelve Steps and shares his or her own experience, strength, and recovery.

4. **Pressure Relief Groups and Pressure Relief Meetings**
   After we have gained some familiarity with the D.A. program, we organize Pressure Relief Groups consisting of ourselves and two other recover-

ing debtors who have not incurred unsecured debt for at least 90 days and who usually have more experience in the program. The group meets in a series of Pressure Relief Meetings to review our financial situation. These meetings typically result in the formulation of a spending plan and an action plan.

5. **Spending Plan**
The spending plan puts our needs first and gives us clarity and balance in our spending. It includes categories for income, spending, debt payment and savings (to help us build cash reserves, however humble). The income plan helps us focus on increasing our income. The debt payment category guides us in making realistic payment arrangements without depriving ourselves. Savings can include prudent reserve, retirement and special purchases.

6. **Action Plan**
With the help of our Pressure Relief Group, we develop a list of specific actions for resolving our debts, improving our financial situation, and achieving our goals without incurring unsecured debt.

7. **The Telephone and the Internet**
We maintain frequent contact with other D.A. members by using the telephone, email, and other forms of communication. We make a point of talking to other D.A. members before and after taking difficult steps in our recovery.

8. **D.A. and A.A. Literature**
We study the literature of Debtors Anonymous and of Alcoholics Anonymous to strengthen our understanding of compulsive disease and of recovery from compulsive debting.

9. **Awareness**
We maintain awareness of the danger of compulsive debt by taking note of bank, loan company, and credit card advertising and their effects on us. We also remain aware of our personal finances in order to avoid vagueness, which can lead to compulsive debting or spending.

10. **Business Meetings**

    We attend business meetings that are held monthly. Many of us have long harbored feelings that "business" was not a part of our lives but for others more qualified. Yet participation in running our own program teaches us how our organization operates, and also helps us to become responsible for our own recovery.

11. **Service**

    We perform service at every level: personal, meeting, Intergroup, and World Service. Service is vital to our recovery. Only through service can we give to others what so generously has been given to us.

12. **Anonymity**

    We practice anonymity, which allows us freedom of expression by assuring us that what we say at meetings or to other D.A. members at any time will not be repeated.

The Twelve Promises of Debtors Anonymous

In the program of Debtors Anonymous, we come together to share our journey in recovering from compulsive debting. There is hope. In working D.A.'s Twelve Steps, we have developed new ways of living. When we work D.A.'s Twelve Steps and use D.A.'s Tools, we begin to receive these gifts of the program:

1. Where once we felt despair, we will experience a newfound hope.

2. Clarity will replace vagueness. Confidence and intuition will replace confusion and chaos. We will live engaged lives, make decisions that best meet our needs, and become the people we were meant to be.

3. We will live within our means, yet our means will not define us.

4. We will begin to live a prosperous life, unencumbered by fear, worry, resentment, or debt.

5. We will realize that we are enough; we will value ourselves and our contributions.

6. Isolation will give way to fellowship; faith will replace fear.

7. We will recognize that there is enough; our resources will be generous and we will share them with others and with D.A.

8. We will cease to compare ourselves to others; jealousy and envy will fade.

9. Acceptance and gratitude will replace regret, self-pity, and longing.

10. We will no longer fear the truth; we will move from hiding in denial to living in reality.

11. Honesty will guide our actions towards a rich life filled with meaning and purpose.

12. We will recognize a Power greater than ourselves as the source of our abundance. We will ask for help and guidance and have faith that they will come.

All this and more is possible. When we work this program with integrity and to the best of our ability, one day at a time, a life of prosperity and serenity will be ours.

Do You Think You Might Be a Compulsive Debtor?

		Yes	No
1.	Are your debts making your home life unhappy?	_____	_____
2.	Does the pressure of your debts distract you from your daily work?	_____	_____
3.	Are your debts affecting your reputation?	_____	_____
4.	Do your debts cause you to think less of yourself?	_____	_____
5.	Have you ever given false information in order to obtain credit?	_____	_____
6.	Have you ever made unrealistic promises to your creditors?	_____	_____
7.	Does the pressure of your debts make you careless of the welfare of your family?	_____	_____
8.	Do you ever fear that your employer, family, or friends will learn the extent of your total indebtedness?	_____	_____

9. When faced with a difficult financial situation, does the prospect of borrowing give you an inordinate feeling of relief? _____ _____

10. Does the pressure of your debts cause you to have difficulty in sleeping? _____ _____

11. Has the pressure of your debts ever caused you to consider getting drunk? _____ _____

12. Have you ever borrowed money without giving adequate consideration to the rate of interest you are required to pay? _____ _____

13. Do you usually expect a negative response when you are subject to a credit investigation? _____ _____

14. Have you ever developed a strict regimen for paying off your debts, only to break it under pressure? _____ _____

15. Do you justify your debts by telling yourself that you are superior to the "other" people, and when you get your "break" you'll be out of debt overnight? _____ _____

How did you score? If you answered yes to eight or more of these questions, the chances are that you have a problem with compulsive debt, or are well on your way to having one.

If this is the case, today can be a turning point in your life. We have all arrived at this crossroad. One road, a soft road, lures people on to further despair, illness, ruin, and in some cases, mental institutions, prison, or suicide. The other road, a more challenging road, leads to self-respect, solvency, healing, and personal fulfillment. We urge you to take the first difficult step onto the more solid road now.

Getting Started

Stop incurring any new unsecured debt.

First and foremost, we suggest that you stop incurring any new unsecured debt, one day at a time. Unsecured debt is any debt not backed up by some form of collateral. Although refraining from compulsive debting may be difficult and painful, it establishes a solid foundation for our recovery.

Attend D.A. meetings regularly.

Attending meetings gives us a sense of hope, an opportunity to identify with others, and a chance to meet people who can help us. Find a meeting in your area.

Record your expenses and your income.

A good way to do this is to buy a small notebook or planner that is easy to carry. Throughout each day, we write down everything we spend and any income we receive, no matter how small the amount. Do not be discouraged if you cannot keep perfect records. If you lose track, begin again as soon as you can. We believe in progress, not perfection.

Read D.A. literature.

You will find useful suggestions and new insights. We also find it helpful to read these books: *A Currency of Hope, Alcoholics Anonymous,* and the *Twelve Steps and Twelve Traditions* of Alcoholics Anonymous.

The Twelve Steps

We suggest that you begin by working the Twelve Steps and by practicing the D.A. Tools. Because we did not arrive overnight at the circumstances that brought us to D.A., solving our problems has required time and effort. While using the Tools of D.A. provides some relief from compulsive debting, working the Steps leads to recovery.

Work the Steps.

We suggest that you work the Twelve Steps in order, preferably with a sponsor or an experienced D.A. member who has worked and continues to work the Steps to the best of his or her ability. For us, true, long-lasting recovery results from a spiritual experience gained by working the Steps.

Step One

We recommend beginning with Step One. The sense of despair or "hitting bottom" we felt when we first came to D.A. was the first step in our recovery. We saw that our own attempts to scheme and manipulate our debts did not work. We admitted that we were powerless over debt. We were ready to ask for help.

Find a sponsor.

To help you work the program, we suggest looking for a sponsor who lives the recovery you want. Sponsors help us work the Twelve Steps, use the D.A. Tools, and carry out our Action Plans.

Ask for a Pressure Relief Meeting.

After you have recorded your income and expenses for (preferably) thirty to forty-five days, attended at least six meetings, and made a commitment to D.A., we suggest that you ask two members of D.A. (usually a man and a woman) to meet with you in a Pressure Relief Meeting. These two D.A. members should have abstained from incurring unsecured debt for at least ninety days and had two Pressure Relief Meetings, and if possible they should have recovery from issues similar to yours. As the members of your Pressure Relief Group, they will help you review your situation and formulate a Spending Plan and an Action Plan.

Anonymity

We suggest that you practice the principle of anonymity. Who we see and what we hear at meetings and in private conversation is kept confidential. This principle allows all members the freedom to speak openly and honestly without fear that our words or deeds may be used to harm us. Please respect the anonymity of all D.A. members.

If you decide that D.A. is not for you, keep us in mind for the future. You are always welcome. Debtors Anonymous will be here when you need it.

Our Stories

1

Reflections on Two Decades
of D.A. Recovery

*An old-timer values the spiritual growth that came
through working the D.A. program.*

As I look back over the two decades that I have been solvent in Debtors Anonymous, I sometimes have to pinch myself to see if I am really here. At the time I found D.A., it had been over a year since I had a permanent address. I was in the process of getting divorced from my first wife, and my own insanity regarding money had contributed to the breakup. I could not recall the last time I had balanced my checkbook, I did not know how many credit cards I had or how much money I owed, and four private credit counselors had not succeeded in changing my ways. I was completely without hope that anything could make a difference.

At D.A. I found people who had been in the same kind of situations I had been in, but had come through to the other side. Now, D.A. was only eleven years old when I found it, and the longest continuous solvency (not incurring new unsecured debt) in the city I was living in was only six years. But that seemed like a lifetime. Here were people who, within a few years of entering D.A., were able to take vacations, buy homes, and live normal lives, without credit cards! For possibly the first time in my life I listened and took their suggestions: come to three meetings a week, keep records, use the other tools (we only had ten tools back then), and work the Twelve Steps of D.A. like my life depended on it. And above all, don't incur any unsecured debt for any reason, NO MATTER WHAT.

I've had a lot of good times and a lot of not-so-good times since then. My first D.A. Fourth Step led to graduate school and earning a doctorate without new debt. I've bought and sold two homes, the second losing a lot of money, but I remained solvent because I had listened when my pressure relief meeting wouldn't accept my rationalization that I didn't really need a prudent reserve! I got remarried, divorced a second time, and married again, the last time to a wonderful lady who is herself a recovering debtor, all without incurring any debt.

My wife and I attend a D.A. couples' issues meeting every week, and it is a new challenge to work D.A. as part of a partnership. (My ego had tried to convince me that I was "pretty good" at working D.A., so I guess my Higher Power decided I needed a dose of humility!) I've lived in large cities and small towns, starting meetings and closing meetings, always keeping the focus on needing to carry the message in order to remind myself of how things used to be when I was an active debtor. Throughout this time, I've looked to old-timers for mentoring, to hear how to live life without debt. Listening, rather than rationalizing, has been essential.

Today I find myself one of those old-timers. And I find the need for that reminder just as great today as when I walked into my first meeting. I have a growing retirement fund, cash in the bank, and live in a nice house in New York City. I sometimes have difficulty relating to newcomers' problems, especially when they ask for advice on specific matters, as it has been many years since I've had to deal with creditors or lacked cash. This is embarrassing, but a good ego deflator, because if I start to think of myself as a D.A. expert, my program is on the path to ruin. And I am reminded that I was once in their shoes, feeling just as hopeless, and that only working the program keeps me from being back in those shoes.

When I tell my story at meetings, I try to let those who are listening know that it is possible to live without unsecured debt, in good times and bad, and that prosperity is available. But the spiritual growth I've experienced is far more valuable than all the material prosperity. I do my little piece, and let God take care of just about everything else. It took me many years in recovery before I developed a regular spiritual practice, but now I go to synagogue almost every morning and pray multiple times each day, a reminder that I am not the source of the good that I experience in life. Expressing gratitude to God and to those who have helped me along the way—those early "old-timers"—is important to my recovery. And I hope that I might give back something; that sharing my own experience, strength, and hope may inspire those who come into the D.A. rooms today.

Originally published in the 2008 second-quarter issue of *Ways & Means* as "A Long-timer Reflects on Two D.A. Decades."

2

From Desperation to
Daily Gratitude

Living a one-day-at-a-time D.A. program for more than twenty years.

On considering my long-term solvency, my first thought is how extremely grateful I am for it. It is a more magnificent gift than I ever dreamed it would be. The only other "experience, strength, and hope" I can share about accruing long-term solvency is that I could only do it one day at a time. Daily, I made a commitment not to incur any new unsecured debt "just for today" for the last twenty-three years and two months. I sought my Higher Power's help in not debting through daily prayer, working D.A.'s Twelve Steps, and "showing up" to the best of my ability. D.A. was, and still is, a one-day-at-a-time program for me.

With the hope that it may be of some service, I will attempt to explain what I was like before D.A. recovery, how I got into recovery, and what I am like now.

Before I came to Debtors Anonymous in 1985, I had just applied for the fourth in a series of $15,000 loans so as to complete the last year of a four-year professional degree program. Prior to those four loans, I had taken four other loans to pay for college and two loans to pay for a graduate program. Additionally, I had incurred several thousand dollars in credit card debt to handle sudden emergencies. I worked full time and went to school at night, yet I was hardly meeting my needs with my salary and certainly did not have funds for school or any extraordinary expenses. In fact, what I thought were "extraordinary" expenses were actually very ordinary expenses, but I lived in a state of deprivation prior to D.A., and did not understand what basic needs were. I was certainly not a "spender," but I was debting to my creditors and to myself.

I was seventeen years old when I took out my first college loan; I was completely vague about the loan's repayment terms and could hardly conceive of the amount that I was borrowing or how difficult it might be to pay it back. I justified taking that loan and subsequent ones because they were for a "good cause"—my education—and I thought that by some sort of alchemy, the degrees that I obtained would translate into financial success. As it states in the chapter on Step Three in A.A.'s *Twelve Steps and Twelve Traditions*, I willfully believed, as other addicts have, that "intelligence, backed by willpower, can rightly control our inner lives and guarantee us success in the world." I did not realize then that I had a disease around money that kept me mired in debt and prevented me from earning a decent living.

I grew up in a large family of limited economic means, where education was not valued, and certainly not for women. Yet, somehow, I seized on the idea that if I could get an education, I might be able to find a legitimate way to escape poverty. Unfortunately, I learned that no amount of knowledge could eradicate my disease of debting. For me, only D.A.'s spiritual solution enabled me to find relief.

When I finished my professional degree, I got a job that paid less than what I was making at the job I had when I was in school. Why? I was a debtor. Most of the people I graduated with were making five times what I made. My diseased thinking about money told me that I did not deserve an adequate salary. I thought that I could not earn more money than my parents did, or I would be betraying my family in a sense, claiming that I was better than them. Yet, I knew then that I did not earn enough to pay back the money that I would soon owe. I had always feared financial insecurity, but suddenly, facing the prospect of having to repay my creditors a staggering several hundred dollars each month once my student loans came due, created a deep desperation in me.

It was that desperation that led me to the rooms of D.A. While I was attending a meeting of another Twelve-Step fellowship, someone shared about

D.A. I had been given the gift of Twelve-Step recovery with regard to another one of my addictions, and upon hearing about D.A., I felt instantly that I belonged. I hoped that it would be able to help me.

In my first year of D.A. I went to one, often two, meetings a day. Although D.A. was then a relatively small program in New York City, I was graced to have several meetings available to me each day. I did not realize it at the time, but I needed to let the program wash over me and be absorbed by me on physical, mental, and spiritual levels; it took me time to understand that my Higher Power wanted me to stop debting, be able to meet my own needs as well as those of my creditors, and learn to live in abundance. I had a lot of very confused ideas about money—more than I realized when I walked into my first D.A. meeting. Yet, at that meeting, I was told to not debt one day at a time, go to meetings, and keep records of my numbers. I was desperate, so I did what was suggested.

I still do not completely understand why or how those actions enabled me to stop debting. For me, that is the spiritual element of D.A.; it worked because I worked it, however imperfectly. I know also that it worked for me because I was working Steps One, Two, and Three at that time. At my first meeting, I admitted that my life had become unmanageable due to my debting. By listening to others at meetings, I came to believe that I, too, could be restored to sanity. Then, somehow, I made a decision to turn my will and my life over to the care of D.A., the Higher Power of my understanding at that time.

After about a year in the program, I got up the courage to ask for a Pressure Relief Meeting. I had almost no idea how to ask for things for myself, and thus that was a very significant turning point for me. With the help of my pressure relief team, I developed a spending plan, negotiated lower payment rates with my creditors, and began to formally work the Steps. It became evident at my Pressure Relief Meetings that I needed to earn more money if I wished to continue to not debt, as my loan payments were coming due. My determination to stay solvent was strong, and I took a part-time job in the evenings as a cashier while continuing to work my real job by day. That was certainly not the success that I thought my education would bring me.

With the extra part-time work, I was able to not incur any new unsecured debt. During those years, I also worked Steps Four, Five, Six, and Seven. Gradually, because I was not debting one day at a time and because I was actively engaged in Step work, I was able to get some clarity that I was hurting others and myself by not securing employment that was commensurate with my abilities and at which I was paid the market rate for my skills. My Pressure Relief Group believed in my ability to earn enough at one job and I committed to them to devote at least ten hours a week to seeking a better full-time job. I took those actions and after months of searching, I finally landed another job at which I earned $20,000 more per year.

Over my years in D.A., I continued to change jobs for better opportunities and better compensation and benefits; I was only able to do so because I was not debting, one day at a time. I was free of the fog of debting and was able to gain enough clarity to begin to acknowledge that I had some value in the workplace. Thus, I began the process of becoming "right-sized."

I also came to understand that as I had taken money from persons and institutions without knowing how or if I could repay it, likewise I had habitually given away my time and services for compensation that was less than adequate. My PRG supported me in being somewhat more adequately paid for my skills and abilities. I would certainly not have been able to ask for adequate compensation for myself if I had not already been working Steps Eight and Nine by making financial amends to my creditors. While I still had not yet overcome my chronic underearning, I began at that time to be able to save, have a prudent reserve, and allow myself to pursue some of my interests, many of which had been lost amidst all the deprivation with which I had lived for so long.

After seventeen years in the program, I paid off my last debt. I followed D.A.'s advice and paid my debts consistently and at amounts that my creditors and I had agreed upon. As I would make those monthly payments, I would often fantasize about what a jubilant day it would be when I surrendered my last debt. In actuality, that day was much more about deep gratitude. I was so grateful to D.A. for showing me a way to make my Ninth Step financial amends by fulfilling my obligations to all of my creditors. I was grateful also for the opportunity to work Steps Ten, Eleven, and Twelve in earnest.

After retiring all of my debt, I began to identify some of my recovery goals or visions. During the first seventeen years of D.A., my vision was to not incur any new unsecured debt, repay my debts in full, and learn to care for myself adequately. Of course, my first and foremost vision continues to be to stay solvent. One other goal that I did identify was to own a successful business. I attended Business Debtors Anonymous meetings and began to build a client base slowly and steadily. I was blessed to achieve that goal in my nineteenth year of recovery.

Then, in late 2006, I met with a new challenge, one I am learning to cope with. Of course, I had had many challenges in my D.A. recovery. Being in D.A. has not meant I found a smooth, straight path to prosperity. There have been fits and starts along the way, yet I have always continued to make slow but definite progress. My current challenge is that I developed a chronic illness, which has prevented me from working the long, workaholic hours to which I was accustomed. I now have to learn to work sanely, and still feel that I deserve to be adequately compensated. While this has been a very difficult time for me, I have been fortunate to be able to remain solvent due to D.A.

Because I work in a very stressful industry, it was suggested to me at a Pressure Relief Meeting many years ago that I purchase disability insurance. I took that suggested action and had the insurance in place for many years when I got sick. That act of planning helped me to be able to remain solvent despite enormous medical costs. I could not have foreseen such an occurrence more than twenty-three years ago. Yet, not debting one day at a time and learning to care for myself in honest and open ways has resulted in many gifts for which I am most grateful, not the least of which is being able to face serious illness with faith and with less fear of economic insecurity than I had when I came to D.A.

Originally published in the 2008 second-quarter issue of *Ways & Means* as "The Twelve Steps Lead from Desperation Debting to Daily Gratitude."

3

A New Way of Life

Disasters brought him to D.A.—and a new life of recovery.

M arch 21, 1996 began as the worst day of my life.
In the early morning hours, my house caught fire and I nearly died trying to escape the smoke and flames in my bedroom. The same afternoon, I was arrested for seven major motor vehicle violations, lost my driver's license, and watched my old junk car being towed away by the police as I stood at the side of a busy U.S. highway.

It was much later I realized that instead of the worst, it had been the best day of my life, because those seeming disasters had brought me face to face with the consequences of my actions as a compulsive debtor, and propelled me at last into Debtors Anonymous. A loving God cared enough about me to hit me "upside the head" so that I could no longer maintain a lifetime of denial and do more damage than I already had to myself and others. Both the house fire and the driving arrest had been directly due to my debting. The utilities in my home had been shut off for nonpayment, and I was trying to live by candlelight in the middle of winter when a candle tipped over and set my bedroom on fire. Similarly, I had not been willing to properly maintain my car for two years, and it had turned unsafe and illegal on me. The registration, insurance, and inspection had expired, and the tires, headlights, brakes, and other equipment were unsafe or completely nonfunctional. These problems of home and automobile were not isolated ones. They were, rather, symbolic of my entire life, which had somehow turned junky, degrading, humiliating, impoverished, and broken without my permission. I had no idea how it had all happened, and was not able to see how a lifetime of spending other people's money and relying on others for basic survival without ever growing up emotionally, spiritually, or financially had made my present circumstances inevitable.

In the aftermath of these two events, I summoned the willingness to make a phone call to a man in another Twelve-Step program, a man who was not a member of Debtors Anonymous but who had learned D.A. principles from friends in another state and used them to overcome problems similar to mine. He became my sponsor and my guide to recovery in D.A. Meeting my sponsor had been another "coincidence" of the type I can only attribute to a Higher Power, because there was not a single D.A. meeting or member of D.A. in my state at this time, and he was the only person for 200 miles in any direction who knew what D.A. was or how it worked. The nearest D.A. meeting was five hours away, and I did not have a car to get to it. I am grateful that my sponsor was a D.A. purist and "Big Book thumper" who took the program literally, and did not mince words with me. He stressed that my life depended on not incurring any unsecured debt one day at a time. I was so terrified and so traumatized from the consequences of years of debting that I became willing to do anything he suggested.

Although I owed more money than I could ever hope to pay back in a lifetime and had always worked at degrading low-wage jobs that barely met my expenses, he insisted that my solvency came first. The first few years were incredibly difficult, but I became solvent right away, lived within my means, paid all my bills on time. Although I was in a great deal of pain, I also began to realize right from the beginning the spiritual transformation that occurs when a compulsive debtor develops the willingness to not debt, one day at a time.

Over the years of my recovery, there have been many miracles. Interestingly, the biggest ones have been emotional and spiritual, rather than purely financial. Although I did succeed in paying off all my debts in an unbelievable five and a half years, and in less than a dozen years I went from someone who was sure he needed to work until age eighty-five just to survive to someone planning a comfortable retirement at sixty-two, those accomplishments seem to be fairly routine in D.A. What is truly miraculous has been the steadily increasing clarity, sanity, and serenity that have compounded like bank interest down through the years, and affected every area of my life. Solvency—continuous, uninterrupted solvency—pays the greatest dividends imaginable, and I believe after almost twelve years (at this writing) that I've barely scratched the surface of my potential in this program. In D.A., I've learned how to meet my real needs. Instead of a house full of unwanted junk bought with credit cards in a never-ending attempt to fill a bottomless hole in me, I am surrounded by an appropriate number of things, possessions I love, use regularly, and maintain in good condition. I've exchanged my debting lifestyle for a savings lifestyle, and I now pay cash for everything. By waiting to research and save for purchases, I have found deep satisfaction in material things, rather than frustration and disappointment in being surrounded by things I'd bought that had failed to "save me." I have experienced the joy of "watching a fellowship grow up around me," as I started the first meeting in my state, then other meetings and an Intergroup. My personal feelings of klutziness and incompetence have yielded to the exhilarating challenges of learning to do service for others on the personal, group, and eventually the World Service levels. I've watched the discipline of keeping D.A. numbers slowly blossom into an inner and outer aesthetic that have taken the form of order and beauty in my home, my yard, my creative work, and the rest of my life. It's difficult to explain to someone who is not solvent the transformation that happens in the life of a compulsive debtor who becomes willing to stop debting. Life somehow becomes transformed from a constant struggle to an opportunity for enjoyment on many levels. When all of my energy is focused on fulfillment rather than fear, I am blessed beyond anything I could have conceived of when I first came to D.A. Maintaining and extending my twelve years of continuous solvency is the most important thing in my life today. I continue to work the Twelve Steps of D.A., and to practice the Twelve Traditions and the Tools. I've found this is a simple program that I no longer need to complicate.

The founder of Debtors Anonymous, John H., once said, "Just get on a cash basis, and everything else will follow." Thank God for the wisdom and insights of John H., and for the catastrophes that brought me to D.A. and gave me the willingness to follow in the footsteps of the recovering debtors who came before us and who have practiced this same set of spiritual principles to recover from this disease for the past thirty-two years.

Originally posted on the Debtors Anonymous website as "Disasters Brought Him D.A.—and a New Way of Life."

4

An Underearner Discovers Real Recovery

"It doesn't matter how much money I earn. I will always be a debtor."

When I first got into D.A. in January of 1995, with a college degree and $20,000 in credit card debt from a self-employment fiasco, I had already cut up my credit cards and cancelled my credit lines. I was writing down my income and expenses (although I had no spending plan), and I thought I had a handle on the whole debting thing. In fact, if you had asked me straight out, I would have said I wasn't really a debtor. I was the one they talk about in the "Twelve Steps of D.A." pamphlet: I came to D.A. "loftily seeking a new perspective on money." I thought I had it all figured out. How hard could it be? I didn't need all that spiritual crap. I thought I'd pay off my debts in two years and leave all you losers behind. I lurked on the fringes of D.A. like a feral cat, hungry for something, but I didn't know what. I had very little awareness of who I was. I didn't want you to know me. I didn't want to know myself. At that stage in my recovery, the idea of admitting my powerlessness over debt, finding a relationship with a Higher Power, and surrendering my will and my life to its care—the first three Steps—was totally inconceivable. This is the story of my odyssey into Twelve-Step recovery.

Step One: What am I powerless over?

I understood Step One intellectually, but not emotionally. Intellectually, I was willing to admit I was powerless, but I wasn't sure exactly over what, considering I didn't really think debting was my problem. I certainly had no emotional concept of what it meant to admit powerlessness, because I was out of touch with every emotion except anger. Rather than truly admit I was defeated, I spent a lot of effort trying to find a label that I felt would adequately describe my unique style of debting. In my early days in D.A., I heard people identify themselves as a variety of things—compulsive debtors, self-debtors, shopaholics, chargeaholics, overspenders, visionaries, underearners, money addicts, committed to prosperity . . . I felt many of the labels described me. When I heard the word "self-debtor," I was like, Yes! Another way to focus everything back on me. And "visionary"! I loved the whole idea of visions, prosperity, abundance—seductive words to one who had lived in deprivation for so long. Now I know that I had no understanding of the cunning disease of debting and how it permeated every aspect of my life. After working the Twelve Steps multiple times, I gradually came to realize my debting disease manifests every time I assume that I am so special I can have whatever I want, whenever I want it, without having to earn it or pay for it. Now I really get that I am powerless over debt.

Step Two: Money was my Higher Power.

Of all the labels I heard at meetings, I was especially enamored with underearner. That label seemed to sum up my life as a wannabe artist. At last I thought I had identified my particular form of the debting disease. More money was the answer. I'd always suspected that money would solve my problems, but once I identified myself as an underearner, I was convinced that earning more money was the solution I'd been searching for. I thought that I was a debtor because I was an underearner. That implied, of course, that if I just earned more money, I wouldn't be a debtor anymore. After a while, I figured out that no matter how much money I had in the bank, I still approached life like a debtor—in other words, self-centered, demanding, vague, and resentful. Clearly, it wasn't about the money.

I've since come to believe that money has as much power over me as I choose to give it. Coming to believe in a Higher Power bigger than money was a long and painful process. I struggled for months, asking all the metaphysical questions D.A.s ask when working Step Two: Is there a God? What is God? Is God a he or a she or an it? Is it something inside me or something external? Can I talk to God like a friend, or is God an impersonal force more like the ocean or the wind? Do I have free will? Or is everything already planned? Is it possible to know the answers to these questions? What if I never find out the answers? Is this all just some colossal joke? I spent a long time distracting myself with endless questions. Finally I moved past the questions to realize that I would never know the answers, simply because I am human, with a human's limited perception and understanding of spiritual matters. What was important was that I kept asking the questions, because that is how I moved closer to a Higher Power I could trust. So, simplistic as it sounds, God or whatever I choose to call it is whatever I need it to be. And when it seems too small, I trade it in for a new, bigger, shinier Higher Power, one that challenges me to keep moving ever closer. Trusting God is not easy for me. I work every day to maintain that spiritual connection. Only a spiritual connection to a Power greater than myself can restore me to sanity.

Step Three: Surrender is the path to serenity.

In a short time, I became disenchanted with the whole visions thing. It wasn't working, and I couldn't figure out why. Didn't God want me to be happy, joyous, and free? Of course, like a true debtor, the only thing that would make me happy was getting my way. Someone suggested I get a sponsor and start working the Steps. I gathered my courage and asked the wrong person to be my sponsor, which of course turned out to be the right person, although you wouldn't have known it at the time. By the time I finished Step Three, my life was falling apart. I tore my life apart by working the Steps. It had to be done, but I didn't know that then. All I could see was my life crumbling around me. I thought there should be a sign over the meeting door warning debtors that if they work the Steps, things will change. And change is not always painless. I quit my job because it was "not a good fit" and thus began a downward spiral of temp jobs punctuated by periods of unemployment. My relationship unraveled, which meant I had to move. I slept on couches and lived out of my car. I kept going to D.A. meetings, and I didn't debt, but I came close. I felt angry and disappointed because my dreams of becoming a famous wealthy artist seemed further away than ever. I lost all sense of self, and finally moved back to my hometown in defeat. I blamed God. It was a type of surrender, maybe, but not a willing surrender. I was still too attached to the payoffs for not surrendering to totally surrender to my Higher Power. I had to understand that placing anything but God in the center of my life always leads me away from my recovery and places me at risk of debting. I began to see that I was receiving many satisfying payoffs for stubbornly choosing self-will: sympathy, attention, and pity were just a few. Every time I work Step Three, I let go of a few more payoffs. Every day I make a decision to surrender everything to the Higher Power, I feel more able to handle life on life's terms.

Steps Four and Five: Honesty and an end to isolation

Back in the hometown in 1997, I found D.A. and began ingratiating myself into the local D.A. community. I became a GSR and attended my first D.A. World Service Conference in 1999. That experience launched my recovery to a new level. I met D.A.s from all over the country and the world, D.A.s who lived full and meaningful lives without debting. I was inspired to work the Steps again. I began to recognize how my attitudes and beliefs were driving my behaviors. Even though I wasn't debting, I responded to people and situations like a debtor. Behind the actual act of incurring unsecured debt was an attitude that affected every part of my life, what amounted to a total life philosophy, an approach to life that was rooted in self-obsession and fear. I was appalled to realize that even though I had not debted since 1994, I was still acting out my debting disease in other ways. My Fourth Steps revealed some of my limiting attitudes and beliefs:

- I realized that I expected to get everything for nothing; I expected to have it all—life, love, work, business meetings, everything—my way, without paying for it, earning it, or contributing my fair share. I had to force myself to arrive early to meetings, to lead when asked, to stay late to put away chairs, to be the Intergroup rep, to say yes to service.

- I learned that I had a fear of taking responsibility for myself, which manifested as an unwillingness to show up for jobs, especially jobs I didn't like or thought I was too good for. I couldn't see myself as a "worker among workers." To retrain my thinking, I started doing service when no one was watching, replacing meeting clocks that mysteriously disappeared, picking up paper towels in restrooms, and downloading and printing copies of the *Ways & Means* to give out free to newcomers.

- I began to see how I used other people's time, money, energy, and possessions, while contributing as little as possible of my own. In my inventory, I chronicled all the times I'd lived with partners and used their stereos, dishes, sheets, furniture, and towels without offering anything of my own because I thought there would never be enough if I gave away what little I had. I was almost fifty before I bought my own television and stereo. My inventory showed me that my whole life I'd been "playing house," too scared to create my own.

- I learned that I was compulsively keeping my life small so it would be "manageable." Fewer zeros were easier to keep track of, fewer things could go wrong. Fewer resources meant the choices were crystal clear: survival mode was the only option. Keeping things small helped me maintain an illusion of control, so I wouldn't have to be afraid.

- I learned I was relying on my record keeping to save me, forgetting that the source of my wholeness and well-being is found in my connection to the Higher Power, which is found through working the Twelve Steps. I thought that if I just had the right spending plan, the right earning plan, or the perfect pressure relief group, that finally I would be safe. I forgot that D.A. is a spiritual program, not a financial management program.

My inventory also revealed to me how my relationship with my parents played an ongoing role in my underearning behaviors. In my family, money equaled love. As long as I was needy and helpless, my parents would express their love for me by giving me money. They wanted me to be safe, because they loved me, and I wanted to feel safe and loved so I accepted their gifts, but the gifts came with both strings and consequences. I felt manipulated and misunderstood, but I also learned to practice self-deceit.

I believe at the core of my debting disease is the attitude that I am special. So special I believe I am exempt from the rules and that I deserve to have everything I want, right now. Or on any given day, so special I deserve to have nothing, not even space on the planet. To me, the essence of my debting behavior is to both undervalue and overvalue my place in the world. Right size was a foreign concept. Either way, my attitudes and behaviors were the manifestation of an ego that was immature, self-centered, unreasonable, irresponsible, and probably supremely annoying. Now I know money is money, and love is love. Only a Power greater than me could remove my shortcomings and transform me into something useful.

Steps Six and Seven: Willingness to be transformed

For a long time I was sad to realize that I held up my "failure" to succeed as an artist as a badge of honor to get attention and ego strokes for my valiant suffering. And further, I spent my energy on dreaming, wanting, and visioning and never got around to the doing. In other words, I didn't work at my craft. It was safer to dream and complain than to take action and risk change. The fear that my art wasn't good enough kept me from improving, thereby creating a self-fulfilling prophecy. As long as I thought money was both the problem and the solution, I kept the spiritual door closed. I had no faith that a Higher Power could be the answer. After all, I asked God for money, and I was given just enough to scrape by. I asked God to let me earn doing something I loved and was presented with crummy jobs that deadened my spirit. God had not proven to be trustworthy in the earning department. As long as I focused on what I wasn't getting from life, I couldn't think about what I could give, thereby closing myself off from the "sunlight of the spirit." When I finally saw all the payoffs I received for not surrendering my earning, my money, and my debting to the care of God, I realized that I wanted to change. I was tired of trying to force life to conform to my demands. I wanted relief from the pain and fear. In Step Six, I became willing to change, and in Step Seven I asked God to change me, and I believe I have been changed. Steps Six and Seven are the transformation steps. Every time I work these steps, I feel like I am changed on a molecular level. I believe God is changing me to the extent I am willing to be changed, shaping me into an instrument that can be of service to God and to my fellows.

Steps Eight and Nine: The gifts and promises of recovery

With the grace of God, I have managed to whittle my list of financial amends down to two transgressions I committed many years ago. When the time is right, I will make these amends. I no longer regret the past, whereas I used to shun it. The harms I've done others and the harms I've done myself are all part of my path, the path that brought me here. Making amends is something I do for me, so I can forgive myself for not being perfect. Self-forgiveness is a necessary step in achieving humility. Thanks to the Steps, I have largely set aside my anxieties over my imperfections. Whenever I feel myself slipping into self-judgment, I ask God to relieve me of the bondage of self; it's my ego that says it is not acceptable to be imperfect. I'm positive God does not judge me as harshly as I judge myself. As a result of working Step Nine, the promises have come true for me: I have clarity, faith, and a newfound hope. My life is satisfyingly rich, filled with meaning and purpose. God has done for me what I could not do for myself.

Step Ten: A new way of living

In 2003, about three months after I paid off my last debt, a job in a completely new field came along. I applied for it and got it. On the same day, coincidentally, I moved into my own apartment for the first time in twenty-five years. I was terrified that life would obliterate me for daring to change, for trying to be self-sufficient, for trying to be big. I white-knuckled my way through those early days, praying to God for guidance and mercy, learning to be the primary adult caregiver in my own life. Slowly I began to settle into a life I could love, with gentle guidance from my Higher Power and the support of the D.A. community. The job paid adequately, and I enjoyed the work. And I had all those things that adults who take responsibility for themselves seem to have: recognition, self-respect, savings, benefits, and a 401(k). In the spirit of Step Ten, I live as mindfully and carefully as I can, one day at a time, to avoid creating situations that I'll have to make amends for later. As of this writing, I am going to graduate school the slow but sane way, paying cash one course at a time. Imagining what comes next both exhilarates and terrifies me—yet another chance to surrender my will and my life to the care of the Higher Power.

Step Eleven: Connection to a spiritual source

The D.A. World Service Conference Convocation is a profound example of how God, the ultimate authority, manifests in the group conscience. It was my privilege to serve D.A. as a trustee. Learning how our organization operates helped me become responsible for my own recovery. When it was time to rotate off the General Service Board, I was delighted to be able to pass the baton of service on to others, so they could have the opportunity to serve D.A. Through giving service, I've learned that God is the path to all that I desire. Instead of focusing on what I lack, I practice gratitude for the gifts I've been given. I've also learned there are many paths to God. My first sponsor used to describe three kinds of prayer. I was trapped in the first two kinds of prayer for years: Help me, God, and F— you, God. That was the best I could do, mired in my anger and self-obsession. Gradually my prayers shifted to a third kind of prayer: Thank you, God. Gratitude inspires me to be a good steward of my own life. Gratitude leads me to Step Twelve.

Step Twelve: Carrying the message into the world

I sometimes hear D.A.s talk about working the Steps as if the outcome will be wealth, fame, and the achievement of their heart's desire. I have learned that the result of working the Steps is a spiritual awakening. In the beginning, that didn't seem like much reward for all the pain and tears. But now I recognize this spiritual awakening as D.A.'s most precious gift to me, because it is the spiritual connection to my Higher Power that allows me to live without debting, one day at a time. I need the D.A. program much more than it needs me. Our common welfare comes first. I'm OK with being anonymous. No one needs to know who I am. For me, it is crucial that I focus my attention on what I can give to life rather than what I can get from it. Remembering that anonymity is a spiritual principle helps me stay out of self-seeking.

Twelve-Step recovery is full of paradoxes: we admit powerlessness to gain true power; we surrender to gain alignment with God's will. Another paradox I've learned is that if I want to keep what I've been given, I must give it away. I love my life now. I don't want to lose it. If D.A. does not survive and thrive, my recovery is at risk. Purely out of a desire to keep what I've been given, I try to focus on being of service in all areas of my life, inside and outside D.A. I have done and continue to do service for D.A. at all levels: personal, meeting, Intergroup, and World Service. Service has been vital to my recovery. Service connected me to God and to my fellows. Considering that my personal recovery depends on the survival of D.A., I always say "yes" to service. I work the Steps with just about anyone who asks, and when we finish Step Twelve, I cut them loose to go out and do the same with others. I also try to focus on being of service outside of D.A. I don't focus on the job, or the paycheck, or the benefits, or even the earning. I focus on being of service. God can do more with me when I am willing to be of service.

In summary, here's what I've learned: (1) It doesn't matter how much money I earn, I will always be a debtor. Sooner or later, if I don't earn, I will eventually debt. After I blow through my savings, retirement funds, home equity line of credit, inheritance, windfall, whatever—if I don't earn, I will debt. It is simple as that. Therefore, I consider underearning to be a symptom of my debting disease, not the cause of it. I underearn because I am a debtor. (2) The only vision worth pursuing is the vision to know and do God's will. Placing any other vision in the center of my life disconnects me from my spiritual source. (3) The greatest gift of working the Steps is the spiritual awakening. I now have a solid faith in a Higher Power I can trust. At last I have an antidote to my doubt and fear.

Thanks to D.A.'s Twelve Steps, no matter what happens in my life, the spiritual source of my well-being and serenity is always available to me should I choose to connect to it. Because of this spiritual awakening, I am not the same person I was when I first came to D.A. seeking a new perspective on money. Through working the Twelve Steps, I found that new perspective and so much more. I have been remade into something I believe God finds more useful. Now I can genuinely say my true vision is to "live usefully and walk humbly under the grace of God."[1]

Originally posted on the Debtors Anonymous website as "An Erstwhile Underearner Discovers the Real Meaning of Recovery."

[1] "Step Twelve," *Twelve Steps and Twelve Traditions*, pp. 124–25.

5

A Twelve-Step Journey out of Debt

A journey from deep debt to "blessings and opportunities."

I have been a grateful member of Debtors Anonymous since 1990. I have abstained from unsecured debt since May 1996, and I have been debt-free since December 1999.

I'm going to share what it's like now, what it was like, and what happened. What is it like now? Thanks to my Higher Power and D.A., I have been granted a practically perfect life. I have only blessings and opportunities, and I live in gratitude through the Twelve-Step way of life.

Besides a small mortgage, I have no debt. I have an excellent job; I earn more than triple what I earned my first year in D.A. I have earned the respect of my professional peers and superiors. This year, my employer has paid my full salary and all expenses for me to attend a prestigious graduate school in a thoroughly prosperous location. My career is poised so that I may soon become a senior executive.

I have been married to a loving wife (second marriages for both of us) for almost fifteen years. I have two delightful stepchildren for whom I have been the loving, caring father they never had before. My stepchildren, now in their thirties, are married to equally delightful spouses. All four are intelligent, good people, building successful professional careers and looking forward to raising happy, prosperous families. With HP's grace, I'll be there to love and enjoy their children—and spoil them rotten!

Since I joined D.A., my wife and I have visited more than twenty countries on six continents. Most recently, we set foot on Antarctica on Christmas Day 2007. We have paid cash for all our trips. We live an abundant life, enjoying the simple everyday things and saving our money to enjoy adventure travel and plan a prosperous retirement. Life is very good, and my cup is always overflowing, never half full.

How is my life imperfect? My imperfections derive from the fact that I am an addict. I create almost all of my problems because I am human and my addict brain wants to relive my inherited "drama" of abandonment, betrayal, and deprivation. I was born into a family descended from five generations of addicts. My father's family of ten children was torn apart when both parents and the oldest child died during the 1918 Spanish flu epidemic. I grew up with thirty-two first cousins from the families of these orphans, almost all of whom were alcoholics, compulsive overeaters, and/or smokers. My addictive personality comes from both nature and nurture.

With this background, what was my life like before I joined D.A.? By the time I joined in 1990, I was $104,000 in debt from eleven "maxed out" credit cards, two major bank loans, and myriad personal debts. I was in the middle of a difficult divorce from an insane first marriage. During this sixteen-year marriage, we went bankrupt in 1975, and we moved twenty-three times (the geographical cure does NOT work!). We borrowed and had not paid tens of thousands of dollars for failed real estate and business ventures.

In July 1990, when my HP miraculously pointed me toward D.A., I had been self-employed for twenty-three years, running a struggling at-home business. I earned only $35,000 that year, the least I had earned since 1978. Importantly, all of these terrible events happened while I was being very successful in a different Twelve-Step program. Abstinent is not sane.

My first five years in D.A. were filled with pain, struggle, and recovery. Despite the pain, I remember those years as full of hope and love. I spent two weeks in a mental hospital for suicidal depression. Both of my parents and my sister-in-law died of lung cancer after long illnesses. The three-year-long divorce finally ended. Only the love and support of my HP, sponsor, program friends, therapist, and significant other carried me through this awful time.

On the positive side, my current wife and I married in a beautiful, debt-free wedding in 1993. I completed graduate school, earning my first masters degree. I began to change careers, doing what I loved to do, rather than what I forced myself to do to pay my creditors. My debt slowly but surely went down, thanks to small monthly payments to my creditors and many large miracles from my HP. By early 1995, my debt had been reduced to $42,000.

Unfortunately, with my new marriage, graduate school, challenging work, and stepchildren, I had begun to slowly drift away from D.A. I became arrogant and launched a grandiose plan to build a million-dollar consulting business by myself in one year. I signed numerous contracts with only a verbal guarantee from a financial backer. In April 1995, my dreams of grandeur were destroyed with one phone call: the guarantor withdrew his support, and instantly I faced $165,000 in unsecured debt.

Within a day, I almost literally crawled back into a D.A. meeting that I had started and begged its few remaining members to take me back. Of course they did. They have been the loving base of support for my rapid recovery and successful life during the past thirteen years. For the next four years, putting my recovery first in my life, I did whatever D.A. told me to do, and for a time, I worked three jobs. Receiving numerous miracles from my HP, I was debt-free by the end of 1999.

In 2002, I joined a large organization, continuing to do what I love to do, and have earned increasing levels of respect and responsibility, increasing my income by 75%.

What happened? What made the difference? I can say only three actions—taken each day—have created my virtually perfect life:

- I am willing, however imperfectly, to do whatever this simple program (and my sponsor, mentors, Pressure Relief Group, and therapist) suggests that I do. I often kick and cuss, but I work the Steps and use the Tools. They work if you work them.

- I give service, service, and more service. I have served D.A. at every level. I continue to do whatever I am asked to do and whatever I can do to be of service. I know that for every hour of service I give, I receive ten hours of recovery; for every dollar I donate, I receive ten dollars in return.

- Most importantly, I seek and do my HP's will for me, as well as I can understand it, one day at a time. That is my only prayer these days: Each morning, I give thanks for all my blessings and ask ONLY for the knowledge and strength to do my HP's will for twenty-four hours.

Finally, I know that I am just another D.A. member. I am an addict with a deadly disease. My feet rest on a foundation of addictive quicksand. My HP's grace arrests my illness one day at a time, and only my HP's love and D.A. raise me from sure destruction and death to the blessed life I lead today.

Originally published in the 2008 fourth-quarter issue of *Ways & Means* as "D.A. + HP: One Member's Formula for 'A Practically Perfect Life'"; revised and posted on the Debtors Anonymous website as "A Twelve Step Journey, from Deep Debt to 'Blessings and Opportunities.'"

6

⁓⁓

Saved by a Power
Greater than Myself

This member exchanged a career of debting for a loan-free college education.

I grew up in a middle-class suburban family that didn't seem all that different from the other families I knew. We didn't talk much about money. I never had an allowance and never really developed a good idea of the relationship between income and expenses.

One thing I do remember is that my parents used credit cards a lot—and for everything, including department store purchases, gasoline, and eating out. Naturally, I assumed that part of being an adult was being able to use plastic money. Little did I know how that attitude would start me on a reckless path of compulsive debting that I could never control.

I started getting credit when I was only seventeen, and therefore not even old enough to be legally responsible for my debts. By the time I was twenty, I had at least a half-dozen credit cards from various department stores and banks, and hundreds of dollars of debt. Nevertheless, I really loved what I thought was the adult-like feeling that charging things gave me. It also was a nice way of saying to the world that I deserved respect, which was important since I had little inherent self-esteem.

For example, I usually traveled using an old backpack, wearing old blue jeans and a flannel shirt. I had a shaggy dark beard and hair over my collar.

Looking like a cross between a hippie and a mass murderer, I would show up in airports and train stations with my backpack and slap my credit card down to pay for my ticket. It was a way of saying, "You may think I'm a bum, but you better respect me since I've got status!"

Once I was out of college and had a job, the credit card offers started rolling in; I accepted all of them, of course. I used credit cards to buy furniture and food, clothing and rental cars. When I got a 25% raise after six months, I figured that there was no reason to worry about debt. Inflation was in double digits, and I assumed that my income would continue to rise. The credit cards could get paid off later with deflated currency.

Two years of this and I had five bank cards, twice that many department store cards, and a new car that I had bought with $200 down, obtained, of course, via a credit card cash advance. My pattern was that I would buy on impulse, especially at sales. Nothing was ever planned, and so I never got anything that cost more than the amount of credit still available on my credit cards. I never really took any nice vacations, or got to see the world, or gave myself any other really nice things that I could remember—that would have taken planning.

The thing that saved me in those early years was that even though I would hit the limits, another creditor would offer me a new credit card or line of credit! Eventually, though, the banks must have realized that I was in over my head and the new preapproved cards stopped coming. I realized it too and saw my first credit counselor—fully six years before I discovered Debtors Anonymous.

The credit counselor did not understand what the problem was. I had a high income, a steady job, and the ability to add up the totals on a budget. She designed a budget for me and politely dismissed me from her office. Oh, if only it were so easy!

Merely using credit totally messed up my cash flow. My bank account was never an accurate reflection of how much money I had available, because I never knew how much money the creditors would ask for when that month's bills came due. Since I often exceeded the credit limits, the entire amount over the limit would need to be paid. I would borrow from one card to pay another. I also loved the "ninety days same as cash" and "six months deferred billing" offers that some stores had. The entire situation was a morass of uncertainty.

I made things worse for myself by putting other people's interests before my own. I was active in politics and got on what seemed like every good-cause mailing list that existed. I was a sucker for the mail order plea for money. And that misplaced generosity extended to my friends and family. One Christmas I pawned my stereo in order to purchase presents for others.

Then things got worse. I lost my job and got married in rapid succession. My wife did not mind me not having an income for a while, and her acceptance of my situation probably blinded me to things I should have noticed that were not working in the relationship. I guess I really needed affirmation. My employment had provided that; now that I was then unemployed, I guess I subconsciously hoped that a relationship could replace my nearly nonexistent self-esteem.

About this time two more credit counselors failed to get me to mend my ways. Debtors Anonymous was still four years away. Actually, in all fairness, the counselors had no idea that this disease really had very little to do with money. I really tried to follow their advice and their very restrictive budget. The deprivation from never being able to buy clothes or eat out was too much to take, however. I was working very hard at a well-paying job and seeing nothing from it. My pattern, repeated several times, was to keep the budget for a few months, then blow it all in one massive unplanned spending binge.

Not that this changed any of my ways! It was at about this time that my then-spouse and I purchased a condominium with no money down—the developer even lent us the money for the closing costs. I totaled my first car and the insurance money was insufficient to pay off the note and get a replacement, so I bought another car with an insufficient down payment. A fourth credit counselor failed to help.

Eventually, our marriage broke up and the expenses mounted up— attorneys, court costs, temporary living expenses. The good thing was that I got into a Twelve-Step program to help me deal with my relationships. I was essentially homeless, moving from one friend's basement to another's living room.

One day I was in a recovery-oriented bookstore and saw a loose-leaf binder with information about lots of different Twelve-Step programs. I leafed through page after page, reading about all kinds of fellowships to help people deal with powerlessness over all kinds of aspects of life—gambling, emotions, drugs, relationships, eating, sex. The Step Twelve advice to "practice these principles in all our affairs" really seemed to have been taken seriously, given the variety of affairs in which people seemed to be using the principles. Each page in the binder had several paragraphs about the particular fellowship, and contact information, both addresses and telephone numbers.

I then came upon an almost empty page. All it said was "Debtors Anonymous" and a telephone number. I had no idea what it was about, but I knew that nothing had ever worked for my spending and debting, and that I was willing to try anything. I copied down the telephone number and called as soon as I got home. A few days later I got a call from a member of D.A. who told me where and when the meetings in the area were held. I attended the first one I could, the first of many, over six years ago.

They told me there were three things I should do. First, I should stop incurring any additional unsecured debt. For me, that meant no more credit cards. Well, I had done that for short periods in the past without any trouble—it was maintaining that abstinence for longer times that was the problem. Nevertheless, I said OK to that one. Second, I was told to come to six meetings in two weeks. I was lucky that there were four meetings each week within three miles of where I lived, and all were on the subway line.

The big problem was the third thing they told me to do. I was instructed to write down in a little notebook every penny I spent and every penny I earned. I had known people who had done this, and my evaluation of them was that they were obsessive control freaks. I had neither the desire nor interest in knowing in such detail what I was spending money on. Years later I can see that my real desire was to maintain my fog of vagueness over all my finances.

Nevertheless, I decided to give it a try. I had already tried four different private credit counselors and knew I couldn't handle this problem myself. I have to remind myself, when newcomers come to D.A. meetings who are reluctant to use the Tools, that many of us must try all the self-will methods before fully admitting powerlessness. I had simply tried them before I had ever heard of Debtors Anonymous. If I had discovered D.A. six years earlier, I don't know whether or not I would have been willing to surrender to the program.

For me, perhaps even more important than the admission of my own powerlessness was that I met people who seemed to have solved their personal spending or debt crises through D.A. What was most striking to me was the number of people who were taking nice vacations—and not just a week at a nearby beach in a crowded run-down beach house! One person was about to go to Rio de Janeiro. Yet another was about to leave for a Caribbean cruise, another had just been to Switzerland and was about to go to Japan, and yet another was saving for a trip the following year to Hong Kong. And everyone was paying in cash! When they shared where they had been financially before D.A., I couldn't believe it. I became willing very quickly to act as if the power of this program could help me—even though it was some time before I really believed it.

About two months later I had my first Pressure Relief Meeting. I was the good little D.A.er and put all of my income and expense recording onto a computer spreadsheet. There was a good and a bad reason for doing this. The good reason is that I tend to sabotage myself with arithmetic errors—and I have a graduate degree in applied mathematics!

The bad reason is that I got a sense of power and control over the numbers by using a computer program. The truth is that the numbers recording income and expense are not there to run and control my life or for me to control or manipulate. The numbers just are. The numbers are just a statement of the truth as to what my values have been for the particular month. It would be some time before I really got this concept deep down. The spending plans I work out in my Pressure Relief Meetings are a prospective look at my values, and the records of what I spend are a retrospective look. When the actual expenditures differ greatly from what I had planned, it means that something is out of control or that I was not telling the truth in the first place about what I valued. And that is it—no judgments attached. I just need to look at why and how my actual spending differs from my plan so that I can correct the situation in the future.

Anyway, I took my eight-inch-high stack of computer printouts into my first Pressure Relief Meeting and the two members of my Pressure Relief Group refused to look at them! They said that I had too much attention on the numbers and not enough on the spiritual side of the program and of life. They had me talk for a long time about what I really wanted in life. Later, they had me make a list of things I wanted in life for myself. At that point, most of the things were material possessions or travel opportunities, since I had been feeling deprived for so long. The biggest ones were to own my own place, to live in a historic building, and to take a trip to Arizona to hike the Grand Canyon. I would learn later that these are examples of what some D.A.ers call visions, and that it is very important to keep these things in mind as we work the day-to-day program. We started on a spending plan that met all these ideals. We put dollar values by each item, but I was instructed not to total the items until the next Pressure Relief Meeting. I came out of that first Pressure Relief Meeting a bit surprised. A Pressure Relief Meeting where I wasn't pressured!

We did add up the numbers in the ideal spending plan at the second Pressure Relief Meeting, and I can see why they did not want me to add them up for myself. The monthly average total for that ideal spending plan was over $1,300 more than my income at the time. They explained to me that I could have anything on the list of ideals (visions) that I wanted, but that I had to plan and that I would not be able to have all of them at once. Well, I was willing to try that, since all of my own efforts had yielded none of them, ever.

A funny thing was happening to me as I continued attending meetings. The desire to use my credit cards disappeared. That first Christmas without debting was tight, but it was a real relief when January came around, and I knew I did not have to worry about surprises in the mail. I started to get a sense that I would get through all this. And I knew it was not me doing it alone. I had the program. I had a Power greater than myself.

Another thing my first Pressure Relief Meeting told me was that I should stop shopping for things on sale. Sales, I was told, encouraged compulsive spending. An amazing thing occurred. I didn't want to go to sales anymore. I was more interested in getting the things on my visions list than in whatever was on sale for what might be the last time. Planning for the larger visions was more important. For the first time, I had a sense that I might get some.

I was also told to stop giving so much to others. Giving is important in D.A.—it is important to feel enough prosperity that I can share it with others. However, what I was doing was giving at the expense of myself. One of the principles, I think, of this program is that there is always enough, and that there will *always* be enough, to go around. My Higher Power will see to it that my needs are taken care of as long as I continue to work the Tools and Steps of this program. My spending plans, developed with my Pressure Relief Group through the inspiration of a Power greater than me, reflect my values as to what I need and want at this time. I can share some of my prosperity—in both time and money—with others, but not at the expense of my own. That is one reason I contribute to the basket every single time it is passed at meetings and why I continue doing service work in my fellowship. I also contribute time and money to my church and occasionally to political candidates I support. But I don't feel that I have to give to every single good cause that finds a way to put my address on its mailing list.

And I have so often seen for myself the fact that there is always enough to go around for so many people that I cannot deny that fact anymore. I have sponsored or done Pressure Relief Groups for people in all walks of life. This includes D.A.ers who have been homeless or who have received public assistance as well as D.A.ers with high six-figure incomes. I have known D.A.ers who could not ever have another checking account or were in legal trouble because of their debts and D.A.ers who were hardly in debt at all, but felt equally out of control. Whatever my problems have been, there has been someone else whose problem, though different from my own, seems even more impossible (to me) to deal with. Nevertheless, that person's Higher Power gets him or her through the difficulties. The only way that I can screw this program up is to think that I've got it licked and don't need D.A. any more.

Within two years of entering D.A., I had started taking some vacations. I purchased a co-op apartment in a historic building with beautiful landscaping on the subway line—and with a real down payment. No more gimmick financing! I began to enjoy some of the endless prosperity that is available, even though I still owed debts. About a year into D.A., I started thinking about lifestyle issues. For example, was the career that was my source of income really rewarding?

About a year and a half into D.A., I really got serious about working the Steps and did my first D.A. Fourth Step. I guess I really didn't want to do it at first—I carried around the A.A. Big Book and an empty pad of paper for several weeks, hoping the inspiration would hit me to start writing. Finally, I was volunteering in the office at a folk festival, monitoring a telephone that nobody ever called, and I started writing to relieve the boredom.

I followed the resentments and fears format described in the Big Book. Lots of resentments came up—toward previous employers, toward schools I had attended, toward people who had lent me money, toward myself. Fears of financial uncertainty also came up. I really liked having a steady income, in what I thought were layoff-proof jobs. Yet, I had sacrificed a lot of my aliveness for security.

What I found was something I had known for a long time but had never admitted to myself. I felt a calling to teach at the university level. I had even taught part-time at a local community college, but to do any more than that required more education. I shared this with some of the local D.A. old timers in a Fifth Step, and they encouraged me to follow my dream. So with that I set out to investigate leaving my career and applying to full-time graduate school—at each step turning over the result to my Higher Power.

I contacted a former professor, who offered encouragement. I obtained the applications and filled them out—letting HP give me the words for the essay. I took the Graduate Record Exam in a roomful of people a decade younger than me—letting HP give me the answers—and did very well. I applied for admission and was accepted. I applied for financial aid and received a full scholarship toward a Ph.D. with the promise of part-time employment. And I took the risk and matriculated—even though I was still in debt. Perhaps most importantly, D.A. gave me the self-esteem to enter a challenging academic program and feel I was worthy of being successful. I've gone to professors' office hours without feeling intimidated. I take examinations expecting to do well. I do research expecting to find the answer.

I sold my co-op with a small profit and moved to a new city, with a new significant other. At the time I applied to that school, there was only one Debtors Anonymous meeting in that new city. I vowed to support the program that had so helped me and to trust my Higher Power to work things out. Today, four years later, there are nine D.A. meetings in the metropolitan area where I attend school.

My significant other and I were married a year into my graduate school. This required new levels of turning life over and even more commitment to work my D.A. program. We planned and had a prosperous wedding and honeymoon with the aid of our Pressure Relief Group and Higher Power. And I still owed debts.

Part of the point is that life does not have to stop until debts are paid. Debtors Anonymous is about living life prosperously one day at a time, regardless of one's financial situation. My debts were finally paid off two years into graduate school and four years into D.A., and there was not much of a difference in my life as a result. My spending plan changed, but my serenity and sense of worth did not. That is because through Debtors Anonymous I had learned that my prosperity, serenity, and spirituality were a function of how well I worked the Steps and Tools, not a function of my bank balance. And this has continued through more recent trials and tribulations: my mother's illness and eventual death, qualifying exams, changing advisors. My concept of God, my Higher Power, keeps changing. Yet no matter how I define it, my Higher Power still seems to work for me and for everyone else I know who works the program.

Today I am in my fourth year of graduate school, writing my dissertation. I am living more prosperously with my graduate student research assistantship than I did in my pre-D.A. days with a yuppie income. Yet the material prosperity of this program is only a small part of recovery.

Through Debtors Anonymous I can deal with any situation, any upset, any problem. I know that with the aid of my Higher Power and my fellow members of D.A., there is no situation in the world that can possibly occur that cannot be handled in a way that my needs are met. This sense of security is not something anybody can take away from me. It is not dependent upon my bank balance, my employer, or any one other individual besides me. It is a sense of security with a drive for control. I can take risks that I once thought were not possible. And even when I screw things up, I can work Step Ten, clean up the mess I made, and rediscover the serenity and peace of this program at once. I can honestly say this program is more valuable than any amount of money in the world.

Originally published in the first edition of *A Currency of Hope*.

7

Building Clarity, Trust, and Joy

Driven to D.A. by the secrets hidden from her spouse, she builds a
relationship of trust and a spirit of service.

I wasn't in a lot of debt when I walked through the doors of D.A., only
around $17,000. I had been in worse debt than that in the past. When I
entered my first Twelve-Step program, I was close to $100,000 in debt, and
that didn't include the condominium that they were threatening to foreclose
on at the time.

I had many reasons for excusing the original debt. At the time, because of
accidents caused by my drinking, I was paying close to $6,000 in car insur-
ance. I had lost my job, twice, and needed the credit cards to exist. But my
favorite came from a radio program that I listened to one day. On it they were
talking about a study they had done on compulsive spending and the use of
Valium. It seemed that when patients were given Valium by their dentists,
they had a habit of compulsively shopping on the way home. Well, with all
the Valium I took, no wonder I racked up so much debt. So after filing for
bankruptcy and losing the condominium to foreclosure, I didn't give my debt
any further thought. I worked on my original program and considered ways
that I could rebuild my credit rating.

About a year after my bankruptcy, I received an offer in the mail to get
a secured credit card. All I needed to do was to send them $100 and they
would give me $500 credit. Perfect! All I had to do was use this card for all

my purchases, pay it off every month, and my credit rating would be restored to its former height. It worked for a while. I even received and was approved for other credit cards with higher lines of credit and no deposit. Eventually, I started leaving a balance on the cards. That was OK, though, as long as I could pay more than the minimum due, right? That's what I thought, anyway.

I continued to spiral out of control. The balances left behind continued to grow until I reached the credit limits. As soon as all my cards reached their limits, I was sent an application for a new card. Thankfully, I wasn't given more than $1,000 on any of the cards, until my last one. They offered me a $5,000 limit. I guess my credit rating was improving! I was no longer able to pay more than the minimum on most cards, and I was continually running out of money before my next paycheck. The cards were no longer a luxury; I needed them to survive. I started making late payments and went over the limit a few times. I would stop spending and bring the debt down a little, then reward myself and watch it go back up.

I received the opportunity to go on some dream vacations during this period, but they were marred by the complicated record keeping I needed to do to make sure that I was never handed a card back because it was declined. So I had all these little notes with the balance on each card and how much credit was left. When I used a card, I would immediately subtract that amount. I hated receiving the "declined" face from store clerks. I wouldn't allow them to ruin my vacation. What a life!

At one of my volunteer jobs I met a really great guy. We dated a few times, and it was soon obvious that this relationship was going to be a little more than casual dating. I almost ran when during one luncheon date he started talking about money, savings, and debt. I felt nauseous. I had never had such a discussion with anyone before. Here he was telling me how much he had in savings and that he had no debt except for a rental property he owned. He didn't even have a mortgage on his house! How was I supposed to tell him that I had no savings to speak of and $7,000 in credit card debt? What would he think of me? Not much, I thought. My throat constricted and my stomach did cartwheels as I got honest about my debt for the first time in my life. Not completely honest, though. I fudged on the totals, which wasn't too hard since I didn't know what I owed for sure. I also conveniently forgot to mention the department store cards that I had.

I was shocked when he offered to pay my cards off and then I could pay him back. That way I didn't have to give them all that money in finance charges. I would close out all cards but one, and use that for emergencies only. It was an offer I couldn't refuse. He wrote out the checks, and I was debt-free. Except for the cards I "forgot" to mention. A couple of weeks later, he started to tell me how proud he was of me for closing out my cards and trying to live on a cash-only basis. All I heard was a voice in my head saying, "Tell him!" I finally got completely honest. Not only did I hide some cards, but I was using the cards that he had paid off to purchase some emergency sweaters, boots, shoes, etc.

I don't think I need to explain the amount of anger and pain that resulted from that revelation. Our relationship nearly ended right then and there. I felt ashamed and worthless. How could I do this to the man I love? I entered the rooms of D.A. in a suicidal depression. I saw no hope for me or our relationship. I prayed every night not to wake up in the morning; I was back to not being able to look at myself in the mirror because of the shame I felt. Even so, I still remember that tiny glimmer of hope that was reignited when I heard the Twelve Signposts for the first time.

I have not incurred any unsecured debt since I first entered the rooms of our beloved fellowship. One thing I heard many times in my other programs was that relapse was NOT a requirement. So I worked this program with that thought in mind from day one.

I started to keep my numbers immediately. Besides meetings, I think that record keeping is the single most important tool that keeps me from overspending. It would really make me stop and think: do I really need this or that for whatever the price was? My spending dropped immediately. I had a couple of Pressure Relief Groups in the beginning months to help me come up with a spending plan, which I still tweak and revise every month. I don't do regular Pressure Relief Groups, though, and really don't believe they are needed. There may be circumstances that require them in my future, but it's my belief that they receive too much attention. I keep close to my Higher Power and the Steps, and that's what keeps me from incurring any unsecured debt.

I still struggled with my spending in the beginning. I didn't debt, but found myself overspending in some categories. I had heard enough in the rooms to know that if I continued, eventually I would debt. I kept hearing people share at meetings about using the envelope system. I hated the thought of it. I saw no reason why I should have to carry around a pile of envelopes stuffed with cash. After continuing to try my way unsuccessfully, I decided to give the envelopes a shot. Let me say I absolutely love the envelope system! I never cared for adding my numbers up every week to see what was left in each category. That left me vague and prone to overspend. With the envelopes, however, all I need to do is see if there is any cash in them. If not, then I know I've spent that month's allotment. And I only have to add my numbers up once a month.

I have received so many gifts from D.A., it's impossible to list them all here, so I'll list the highlights. After a rough first year, my relationship improved and I earned back the trust that I had lost. He proposed, and I was able to have the wedding of my dreams, paid for in cash. I have discovered within myself a creativity I never knew existed. I have found enjoyment in writing and hope to be published one day. I've also discovered a joy in expressing myself through jewelry designs. My materials and design are unusual and not for everyone, but they are most definitely me.

I've discovered a whole new understanding of my Higher Power. It may not be conventional, but it fits who I am today. Since I've become more comfortable in my skin, I'm less concerned if others find me odd, and that gives me a whole new freedom. I am most grateful for the chance to do service. It can be hard work sometimes, but always rewarding. I've met some wonderful people who share my love for this program and who help me to learn and to grow. I'm grateful for the pain that brought me into D.A. and for the people who held the doors open for me.

I'm grateful for the opportunity that I've been given to hold that door open for the next sick and suffering debtor.

Originally posted on the Debtors Anonymous website as "Building Clarity, Trust, and Joy, the D.A. Way."

8

~

An Unlikely Debtor

"I'm a compulsive debtor. When I admit that, my life moves forward."

I don't "look like" a debtor. That was the story of my life. That's how I got into Debtors Anonymous.

I was the first of five kids of alcoholic parents. I was the first one to go to college. I was the only one in my whole family who had ever gone to college. I was very self-reliant. I could present myself like someone who didn't have problems. I was a Jewish kid raised Catholic. I was half white, half Spanish. I could pass for white; I could pass for Gentile; I could pass for rich.

I got out of professional school in 1975. When I was a kid my dad told me at eight years old, "You're a smart little boy, but I don't have any money and you're going to have to get yourself to high school and you'll have to get yourself through college. You'll have to get a scholarship and you need to be a doctor, dentist, or a lawyer and you won't have any problems, because they didn't have any problems during the Depression." Those were the choices—a doctor, dentist, or lawyer. My real joy was animals, my real joy was plants, and my real joy was music, but that didn't matter. "That's fine, son, but you need to be a doctor, dentist, or lawyer." As a kid I would always do gardening—I wanted to be a landscape architect. "Nope, doctor, dentist, or lawyer."

I went to professional school. When I got out of school, my dad told me, "You can do anything you want to do; you can do whatever you want." While I was in school, I would get student loans. I would sign for those loans as if it was no problem. I knew it would take a long time to pay them off, but I'd think to myself, "Oh, no problem." At school, my lab partner told me, "They've got this new thing—you can get a $50 credit card—you need to get this and you need to get good credit." So I signed up for a credit card. I also had loans and grants and I started using my loans to go on vacation. I'd go to Hawaii or I'd go to San Francisco because I deserved it. I was working hard. By the time I got out of school I didn't even know how much money I owed. I found the paperwork and in 1975 I owed $139,000 in unsecured debt. In 1975, $139,000 was a LOT of money.

I started working, and when I got out of school I got my license. I worked ten weeks and when I went to the IRS to get tax paperwork, the IRS employee helping me asked, "Now, do you think you're going to make the same amount of money next year?" I had no idea what I would make or what I would owe, but after all, you can't keep the government's money. I had forgotten about taxes.

By the time I discovered the Twelve Steps, it was 1975. I had married an alcoholic and found a support group for people in relationships with alcoholics. I started going to those meetings—I remember hearing them tell me to try it for six months, not six meetings—six months! They told me that if I didn't like what I found there they would gladly refund my misery. By then I was agoraphobic—I didn't want to leave the house—and I knew that was pretty bad. I was a psychology major—I knew that was not good.

I started working, and what was overwhelming to me was that I was living on a thousand dollars. I was paying $3,000 a month to pay off my loans. I had a crappy car. I had a crappy apartment. I was making $48,000 a year, but the income tax on that was another $26,000, so I had to make more than $70,000 a year to live on $1,000 a month.

I got nice clothes with my credit card because I deserved it. I parked my car four blocks away so you'd never see it. I never brought anyone home to my house—I stayed at their house. In 1978 I found a new support group for people who had been in relationships with alcoholics, and I went to seminars of the people who actually wrote very famous books about this. I was learning a lot about this experience and I could see the patterns that had developed in my life.

I mentioned earlier that I had always been very self-reliant. It was true, but I didn't get myself to D.A. on my own. I got to D.A. in 1982 because someone in this program directed me here. Her name was Lila B., and I will always be grateful to her for her guidance. I'd go to those other meetings and seminars and run into Lila. She'd ask how I was doing and I'd tell her, "God, I never have any money. I'm making money, but I never have any money." Lila told me, "I've I got the program for you."

I had heard the Promises of A.A. before, and every time I heard "Fear of people and of economic insecurity will leave us" I'd say, "Oh, god, I feel so much pressure." So I finally went to the D.A. meeting and there was no one there. By this point I was divorced and my girlfriend asked, "How was the meeting?" I told her, "Well, those damned Twelve-Step people, they're so irresponsible; there was nobody there at that meeting. Nobody!" Later, when I asked Lila what happened, she told me, "Oh, that was not a prosperous place and we needed to have a prosperous place."

So the next time I went I had to go across town—an hour's drive—to this beautiful library. I went, but I could only go every other week. My experience is that every other week just doesn't work. Finally the day got changed to a Wednesday, and I could go every week. At first, I didn't say I was a compulsive debtor—no, no, no, no, no! It was as if I was going to A.A. and telling them, "I'm a light beer drinker! I'm a champagne cocktail drinker!" In D.A. I was telling them, "I'm not a debtor, I'm a compulsive shopper. Look—I have nice things. I can afford nice things. I can afford to buy nice things. I'm not a compulsive debtor."

I shared like that for a year until the founder of D.A. came from New York and kindly revealed the truth to me. He and others, through sharing their own experience, let me know that I could claim to be a compulsive shopper, but I was in fact a compulsive debtor, and that when I started acknowledging that, my life would change. I surrendered, and they were right.

I've been going to D.A. for twenty-four years now and I've heard a lot of different buzzwords over the years. Now I hear "underearner." That sounds pretty cool. I also hear "deprivation addict." But I'm a compulsive debtor. When I admit that, my life moves forward.

It took me a year and a half to quit using my credit cards. I had never had a Pressure Relief Group. The only reason I finally did a Pressure Relief Group was that there were only seven people in D.A. in Los Angeles, and the other six finally noticed. Since they were the only members, they knew they had never done a PRG for me. I did it, finally. It was a little scary—actually, it was really scary—and I didn't do another one for a couple of years.

As time went on, what I learned in the program was that it is about the Steps. I paid off my debts in seven years. I didn't get an award for that. It wasn't like someone told me, "Oh, you're so fabulous, your picture's in the paper—you just paid off your debt!" What I learned was that debting was a disease of impatience. I didn't want to wait anymore. I wanted mine right now. When I put that card down I could get it right now. I was tired of waiting. So my debt had grown to $180,000 and I had to sell my house—it was really a pretty powerful time. I didn't get into D.A. and really start doing it until I was thirty-two years old. I didn't have a car, I didn't have a house, but I had nice clothes. I debted buying beautiful suits and a lot of greeting cards. I had so many suits—I had winter suits and spring suits and East Coast suits and Hawaii suits, and one day someone broke into my apartment and stole all my suits. I guess the thief wanted to look good, too. He wanted to pass for rich.

So I got to D.A., and learned to identify as a compulsive debtor. I learned to do service. You know, we started so small, it took forever to get any meetings going. We found new members in other Twelve-Step groups, and that's how the program started growing. The thing is that it just takes a little bit at a time. I saw people come and go, old-timers who didn't think they needed it anymore, but I always had the example of Lila—she always kept coming. She told me the story of her and another member. They sat in a room across from each other for a whole year, not really liking each other, but committed to the program and to recovery. I wondered why they would do that, but now I know they were trusting the process. They were showing up and showing up and showing up.

I have had different milestones in my recovery in D.A. I realized what really helped me was getting started having Pressure Relief Groups and doing them every two months. I started looking around the room and saying, "Hey, these people are doing pretty good and I'm just stuck, I'm just stuck"—because I wasn't working the Tools. Over time I worked the Steps and the Tools. I learned to identify as a compulsive debtor—this isn't a shopping thing. It is a disease that kills. It is a disease, it really, really is.

I've learned to be of service in D.A. I hear about others who feel alone in recovery, but I don't feel like that in D.A. I'm a General Service Representative and I sponsor others and I don't feel alone. I work the Steps and encourage others to do so. I've learned to do things the D.A. way. It works for me to use the Steps and the Tools and it works to keep the focus on the debtor who still suffers.

I learned from Lila to have a prosperity consciousness. She taught me to dare to have a bigger life and write it down. When I've been willing to do that (like today when I did a vision board) I live out what I write down. I heard there is life after debt, and I've learned there really is.

I've learned to get really clear—how can I be the best man I'm supposed to be today? That's what I ask everyday: "God is my Source, and how can I be the best man I'm supposed to be and how can I shine or share my light with others?" When I'm willing to share my light with others, I prosper. I spent quite a bit of my life wanting to keep a distance between myself and other people, but that's not God's vision for me. I prosper when I'm out with people and sharing with people. I encourage all of you to shine and to share your light and realize that God is the Source, and to affirm every day, "I want a bigger life."

Originally posted on the Debtors Anonymous website as "An 'Unlikely' Debtor Learns to Share His Light in D.A."

9

There's a Monster Living inside Me

"When I lost my first tooth, the tooth fairy left an I.O.U. under my pillow."

There's a monster living inside me, and I call him "Not Enough." Every time I try to feed him he screams, "I want more stuff!" A bike, nice clothes, new furniture, some pretty jewelry, vacations all around the world, all sorts of niceties. These things and more I've used to quench his beastly appetite. I finally shrug and tell myself I've tried with all my might. Then I plan to ignore him when he starts his usual stuff, but he screams more loudly, "Hey! It's *you* who's 'Not Enough.'" My only ammunition in dealing with this jerk is what I call my Higher Power, and boy, does it work!! I say, "HP, I need your help. Please shut up this big ape." HP sits me on his lap and asks, "Child, when will you see that the only way to quiet this goon is to fill him full of me!"

I now suspect the true monster was driving the first ten years of my life, which I remember as being very deprived. My father was in pharmacy school, while my mother worked as a secretary. We were on welfare, so poor that when I lost my first tooth, the tooth fairy had to leave an I.O.U. under my pillow. My parents had searched the house from top to bottom to find even a penny, and after a fruitless search between couch seats and car ashtrays, they had to leave an I.O.U. for me. My father borrowed a nickel from a classmate and placed it under my pillow the next night. Thus, my introduction to debting. Living under such deprived conditions, I was constantly aware of there not being enough.

Our basic living needs were barely met. This standard of living continued until my Dad graduated from college. We went from deprivation to abundance almost overnight. Suddenly there was money to spend frivolously. Throughout my adolescence I held various odd jobs, and just as soon as I got paid I spent my entire paycheck. When I'd ask my parents for more money, they would exclaim, "You just got paid; what happened to your paycheck?" I didn't have a clue where my money went. It just seemed to slip through my fingers. This vagueness was one of the main characteristics of my debting years. I never knew where my money went. I could withdraw $40 from the bank and the very next day be broke, wondering what had happened to it. And I never learned the value of saving. It was as though there was a monster in me that needed immediate gratification. Tomorrow wouldn't do; the monster needed more and more, and it needed it now. I waited tables to put myself through college, all the while becoming more vague about my money.

I took out a student loan and was approved, but instead of using the money to cover living expenses, I squandered it on material things. Upon graduating from college, I was approved for two credit cards and thus began my descent into hell. I started charging things left and right, ignoring the bills as they came. Soon came the harassing phone calls from creditors. The phone became my enemy; I dreaded hearing it ring. I was so stressed out that I eventually wouldn't answer it, or I would answer and pretend to be somebody else. Now that's insanity . . . taking messages for myself to avoid dealing with reality!

Things went from horrible to excruciating until I finally decided to move across the country to "start new." In Twelve-Step programs, this is known as a geographic cure. My parents, being enablers, refused to let me file bankruptcy though I was twenty-seven at the time. They agreed to pay off my debt with the understanding that I would pay them back when I was able. I consented, but still moved from New Orleans to San Francisco to "start fresh." Although I was unable to accrue more debt from credit cards, I began to debt myself in other ways: underearning, underachieving, putting others' needs ahead of my own, while I neglected my own. I even "borrowed" from the treasury of the Twelve-Step group I was doing service for. My "fresh start" soon became the same old, same old.

Finally I had had enough. I went to D.A. and sat quietly while others talked. I was amazed at how much I identified with those who shared. I began working my D.A. program. I felt like a newcomer, even though I had been clean and sober for over six years. I began writing down my daily expenses on the first of January, a few months after coming to D.A. I immediately noticed that the vagueness that had plagued me for years vanished. I began feeling hope.

I formed a Pressure Relief Group, and a most incredible miracle occurred: I quit worrying about money. Somehow I realized that I would be OK, one day at a time. My Higher Power is taking care of me, and as long as I continue to take action and do the footwork, I will make it through anything. Nine months after coming to D.A., I got a higher-paying job. I have been having regular Pressure Relief Groups and have been participating in others' since my third month in this program. I have approached my family to make amends for my debting. I've retired some debts. And I'm learning how to put my needs ahead of others, especially that "ogre that wants immediate gratification."

In a nutshell, I am learning how to be a responsible, productive adult human being for the first time in my life. D.A. is a program of action, and I have found that service work is a good way to keep me connected to the program; it keeps me active. This program has shown me that the universe is abundant and that I am worthy of my portion of that abundance: All I have to do is claim it! Lastly and most important, D.A. has reminded me of my visions and dreams for myself.

D.A. has given those back with the message that the only thing preventing me from realizing my dreams is me. The gratitude I have for Debtors Anonymous is enormous. Thank God for D.A.!

Originally published in the first edition of *A Currency of Hope.*

10

Thank God for a Long, Slow Recovery

Crises are replaced with unexpected boons as this debtor develops faith.

I walked into my first D.A. meeting in 1990 at St. Bart's Church in Manhattan on a Saturday in July. A week before, I had bought what I professed to be my last credit card purchase—a new $40 wristwatch on a department store account. I reasoned that, once I had joined D.A., "they" wouldn't let me use my credit cards anymore. And since I didn't have enough money to buy a new watch, and needed one, I figured I'd better squeeze this last one in.

A few months earlier, I had read a financial self-help book that tactfully suggested that if one chronically owed more than 10% of one's total income "you might want to check out Debtors Anonymous." There I was in New York City, supporting my wife and infant son on an annual salary of $23,000, more than $34,000 in debt without the income to keep up with even minimal payments: defaulted on two student loans, bank credit cards all maxed out, department store cards maxed out, behind on gas card payments, two months behind on my rent, behind on all my utilities, in debt to my shrink, in debt to my parents, and maxed out on borrowing from friends and family. We were reduced to digging around the crevices of the couch for loose change. Collection agencies were aggressively calling at home and at work—my stomach turned every time the phone rang.

Trying D.A. seemed like a good idea, but Twelve-Step programs made me nervous with all that God talk. This lifelong atheist had a hard time with that, but I was pretty desperate and didn't have anywhere else to turn. I was lucky; I had bottomed out. But it took me three months to finally show up. From the moment I started listening to others share, I knew I was in the right place. I attended six meetings, as suggested, and I listened. At my fifth meeting, I shared about my desperate situation—I barely had enough money for a subway token to work the next day. Several people shoved notes toward me with their phone numbers. One woman had attached a subway token, saying that someone had done that for her when she first came in, and she was passing it along. After the meeting, I went to a phone booth to call my wife and about two bucks worth of quarters came tinkling into the coin return.

Not long after, I asked a man and a woman to do a Pressure Relief Meeting for me. I'll never forget that night, attending New York's largest meeting in a pouring rain, the room packed with debtors, and the sweet cleansing after-the-rain feeling as we left that meeting for mine. They helped me work out an emergency spending plan (I recall filling only about half a page with categories at that time), and they helped me work out an action plan to contact all my creditors. I worked out payment plans with my utilities and landlord, and I informed the others that I was unable to pay anything at that time but would contact them every three months to update them on my situation—a moratorium. (I needed to take care of myself before taking care of them.) And they urged me to cut up all my credit cards and commit to not incurring any further unsecured debt, one day at a time, no matter what. Of course I thought I had to debt because of my dire circumstances. But that watch became my final credit card purchase, and I started to stay current on paying my bills—even when it was scary to do so.

I also realized that I needed to separate financially from my wife. I went into that D.A. meeting thinking that "we" had a problem with debt. I walked out of the meeting realizing that I was a compulsive debtor and that I didn't need to do her inventory. Since she didn't earn an income, she became a category in my spending plan—and I let go of what she did with that money. As she had always balanced the checkbook, I explained to her that I needed to take it on myself so I could be responsible for my own recovery. And I took responsibility for paying all our bills.

Not long before I read about D.A., I had read about prosperity conscious-ness in a number of self-help books, which helped me begin to become aware of how I tended to live my life in deprivation. So I tried pushing myself at the department store on "Wednesday sale night" by spending a bit more on designer shirts or underwear instead of always going for the cheapo brands. (Every Wednesday seemed like the absolute LAST CHANCE to take advan-tage of these great deals.) The new behavior was exhilarating, but there was one big problem. I didn't "spend" anything; I just went deeper into debt. While I practiced what seemed to me like a healthy new behavior, I dug a deeper and deeper hole. I would not and could not let go of my own money to buy these things.

There was a meeting I attended after about a year in D.A. when I sudden-ly realized that everything I was wearing, from my underwear to that watch, from my shoes to my briefcase, had been purchased with credit cards and hadn't been paid for. After about another year of not incurring new unsecured debt one day at a time, I attended the same meeting with the sudden realiza-tion—and great satisfaction—that everything on me had been paid for in cash. It became clear to me that abundance and prosperity could only come to me if I did not debt one day at a time.

After I joined D.A., I conscientiously started practicing the Tools. I used to love the old opening of the D.A. Tools that said "action is the magic word." I can isolate and procrastinate and get nowhere, or I can keep taking actions that move me forward. When I found that I wasn't practicing one of the Tools, I would make an effort to shift my focus to it. Early on, I started keeping my numbers to the penny. Even today, when I make a purchase, I literally go into a blackout and have no recollection of what I've just spent if I don't make a note of it. Record keeping provides for me a kind of spiritual discipline in which I create a consciousness about my spending that never existed before.

For me, all the Tools help me practice new behaviors. Using the telephone taught me to ask for help—in communicating with creditors, dealing with panic, and just checking in instead of isolating. I also discovered other things about myself. I had collected some phone numbers from a few women in the rooms, and one day one of them asked me, "Do you ever call any men in the program?" The answer was no; the idea of asking other men for help was very hard for me. She suggested I walk up to three men at the end of each meeting and ask for their phone numbers. I did and have been blessed with the support of incredible male sponsors and program friends ever since.

The Tools helped me get my feet on the ground so that I could begin to let in the spirituality of the program. I got myself a sponsor and began working the Steps. When he suggested I do a ninety-and-ninety—that is, attend ninety meetings within ninety days—I did so. It was a deeply spiritual experience for me as I committed myself to our program and began to feel the presence of a Higher Power in my recovery and life. And I read the A.A. *Twelve Steps and Twelve Traditions* and the A.A. "Big Book" regularly and began underlining the parts that popped out for me.

Through the Steps, I began to shine the light on my past behaviors. I found a pattern in my life of dependence on others, a penchant for seeking something for nothing, and stealing from my parents and my employers. I stole because I never felt like I had enough. I used credit cards because I wasn't willing to spend my own money on anything. I could only buy things with the "free money" promised through credit cards. And I had to admit, I NEVER really intended to pay any of it back; I always thought some magic would occur that would just take care of it all.

While some people come into D.A. as "big-shot spenders," I experienced the opposite. I never turned down a free meal and tended to allow others to treat me rather than the other way around. When I stayed in a hotel, I found it difficult to check out without taking the shampoo and soap with me. I eventually began to practice acting different by turning down free things to buy them myself, insisting on paying the restaurant bill when I ate with my parents or brothers (within my spending plan), and resisting "free samples." I remember attending a professional meeting that promised a free lunch. I literally had to tear myself away to attend a D.A. meeting instead, buying my own lunch along the way. It was a strange new behavior for me.

I also realized that I had a pattern of underearning. My first job out of college was at McDonald's, flipping burgers. After four years of art school, an acquaintance hired me to do a drawing for her organization and asked me how much I'd charge. I replied, "Ten bucks." I had no sense of my earning power—I was literally clueless about asking for what I needed. And I realized that I had equated incurring debt with being "grown up." I remember coming to the conclusion that people walked into car dealerships and bought cars on credit, so I did the same—but with absolutely no clarity about whether I made enough to afford the payments. So I quit my job at the post office and paid the car off in full with my retirement money. (Retirement? Never gave that any thought.) I quit that job to go back to graduate school, and student loans took me in way over my head. But then I took a job for two years in China, where they couldn't find me. I even found a way to get my department head to support my claim that I shouldn't be expected to repay yet on my annual salary of $3,500 in China. (No, that isn't missing a zero.) When I returned to New York, they found me—and the final slide began.

After I had kept my numbers for several months and started putting them into spreadsheets, my Pressure Group looked over my records and announced, "You need to increase your income." I of course expected them to tell me I needed to spend less and deprive myself more. It really pissed me off. I didn't think I was capable of earning more—after all, I had a respectable job directing a continuing education program. But they urged me to make a list of ways I could increase my income right away. This led to my doing private tutoring, completing a textbook I was contracted to write in a year (but which I procrastinated on for three), and reviewing new book proposals for an educational publisher.

In the meantime, my creditors weren't happy with my moratorium, so the harassment increased. Through someone's suggestion, I asked my creditors—in writing—to contact me only by mail. When creditors called anyway, I followed a script: "I understand that you have a procedure to follow. I take full responsibility for this debt, and I have every intention of paying it back in full. However, I am unable to make any payments at this time. I will contact you in three months and let you know if my situation has changed." No matter what they came back to me with (and often they were pretty abusive), I repeated those lines like a broken record. The invasive phone calls began to decrease and eventually stopped altogether.

After a year and a half moratorium, as my income slowly increased, I began debt repayment, making small payments according to the percentage each creditor represented of my total debt. Some got as little as a dollar—the largest got $50. Eventually, the total amount of my debt repayment continued to increase, as my income increased, to $350 a month. My creditors, of course, were never satisfied. Three of them took me to court. I negotiated a payment plan in the courtroom with two. In the small miracles typical in this program, my income increased just enough so that I had the money I needed. The third creditor was very kind to me over the phone, so when they told me to sign the forms they were sending me, I dutifully did so and suddenly found myself with a judgment against me which led to my wages getting garnished. (I had forgotten to call someone in program first.) With program support, I called the city marshal and negotiated a payment plan, which lifted the order. Later, they froze my bank account the day before Christmas (I had just a few dollars in my pocket). The day after, I contacted the creditor and negotiated a payment plan that unfroze the account. I was learning to face the "bogeyman" again and again—situations that I had had no idea how to deal with before coming to D.A. and had been willing to do anything to avoid. But now I was facing them—and overcoming them—one day at a time.

About a year later, my young son tripped and fell on some very rough sidewalk in front of the department store that had garnished my wages. He required stitches on his chin and my wife responded by calling a lawyer, which really made me squirm. However, my time in the rooms helped me to let go and not meddle with her stuff. (I reached a place of clarity, realizing that department stores have insurance and a procedure to follow in such circumstances.) Her action led to a judgment in which my son received a sum equal to the amount I had owed in unsecured debt to that store, which sat locked in a bank account until he was college age.

With the actions I took from my Pressure Relief Meetings, I slowly increased my income, and one—the publisher's reviews—led to a job offer from that publisher, doubling my original salary. At first, they offered me $45,000, but I spoke with my sponsor, asked for $50,000, and got it. For me, this alone was a miracle, as I had always imagined I was incapable of earning any more than $35,000—a self-imposed ceiling. As a matter of fact, I thought if I made $35,000, I'd have it made (which was insane). In addition, the job included extensive travel, which had always been a dream of mine. At the same time, my textbook got published and started bringing in a steady $10,000 a year in royalties.

After a couple of years, I came to realize that I had developed experience and skills that were attractive to other companies and I explored some options. But I realized that I wanted to stay where I was, so I decided to ask for a raise. With my $35,000 mental block, it brought up a lot of fear, and I had to share at meetings and use the telephone to turn it over in order to calm the feelings. My sponsor encouraged me to take the action even if I felt the fear. After about three months, I bookended with him that I was ready. As he suggested, I left my office by taking baby steps toward my boss's office. I literally watched my feet taking the steps as I walked down the hall. I asked, even though I felt like my voice was shaking, and my boss agreed.

Over time, I came to refer to "God" in my recovery and continue to do so today. I do so without being in the least bit religious. I feel like God has a plan for me and that my job is to show up and let it happen. And I've made prayer a regular part of my life, always ending with "Thy will, not mine, be done." If I'm not willing to NOT have what I pray for, then I know I'm doing something wrong. For me, the Steps are central to applying spiritual principles in my life for my own recovery. I've learned that it's important for me to make amends for my own benefit. One day, after several years in program, I found myself stealing a magazine from my dentist's office with my young son by my side (it had an article on debt and I felt entitled). That really made me feel ashamed, and when I got home I immediately called my sponsor. He suggested I go back to my dentist and tell him, and that I make a donation of $10 toward a patient who could use it. My dentist thought I was nuts ("I don't know what church you're going to, but you can keep the magazine.") I returned it and gave $10 to his receptionist. It was a rigorous honesty I had to "practice" for my own recovery.

I also learned about gift giving. At first, I had to spend a lot less on gifts in order to stay within my spending plan. So I learned to give and let go. Because I never thought I had enough, receiving gifts had also always been problematic for me. Through the program, I've learned to believe that I always have enough. And I've learned that I can provide for myself instead of expecting others to fill that hole for me. I also learned over time—as someone who was accustomed to deprivation—how to spend more money on gifts for myself and my immediate family. One action my Pressure Relief Group gave me was to go to Tiffany's and get my wife a gift for up to $250. I took my young son with me, who whined the whole time about how bored he was. The store made me uncomfortable, but I looked until I found a couple of potential gold pieces. When I couldn't make a decision, I asked for my son's opinion. He stopped whining just long enough to point at one. When I asked why, he answered with childlike wisdom, "Because it's unique." He was right—she loved it. Around gifts, I've learned to spend appropriately, give, and let go.

After a number of years in D.A., I found myself with a vision to buy a car, and house in the Hudson River Valley. (Until then, I could only imagine one vision: to not incur any new unsecured debt no matter what.) I had gone twelve years in New York without a car—not because New Yorkers don't drive, but because I didn't think I could afford one. Also, I had so much shame about my debts that it was difficult to go through the process. My Pressure Relief Group helped me take baby steps toward buying one, and I ended up getting a car that was much nicer than I had ever allowed myself to have in the past.

In the early nineties, our landlord had left the country and allowed our small building to fall into disrepair. (One night my wife and I were horrified to feel cockroaches running across us in bed.) I didn't think buying a house would ever be possible for me because of the moratorium I had taken on debt repayment. But my Pressure Relief Group encouraged me to take actions anyway. The new car allowed my wife and I to drive out of the city and start looking. We soon found the "perfect" house, but thanks to the program I was able to see that the price was above my spending plan—and therefore not perfect at all. Despite feeling discouraged by all the crappy houses that were listed at our price range, we continued to look. After about a year, we found a beautiful 1929 house that we both fell in love with. When I called the mortgage guy, I decided to be honest, rather than hide in the shame. I warned him that I had defaulted on my loans in 1990, so he checked my history. In a few minutes he got back on the phone and exclaimed, "Your credit rating is excellent!"

An amazing thing for me is that for every difficult or overwhelming suggestion I've taken in this program, I would eventually find the faith to show up and let the good in—and my income would increase at just the right time. Shortly after closing on the house, I was promoted to an executive position with a corner office and a six-figure salary. The promotion scared the heck out of me and there were numerous times when I had to shut my door and use the telephone just to keep my sanity. But the program has taught me to put one foot in front of the other, and to recognize that panic is deadly. Using the telephone and the Steps helps me overcome panic and keep moving forward, so that's what I do.

The Twelfth Step—carrying the message and doing service—has been a key part of recovery for me. I've volunteered to be secretary, treasurer, literature chair, and meeting chair for the various meetings I've attended—not because

I wanted to help out, but because I was selfish and wanted to recover. At one point, I heard that someone was needed to publish the New York Intergroup newsletter, which had been falling behind in its publication, and I attended the monthly Intergroup meeting and volunteered. Two years later, hearing that someone was needed as special events coordinator, I volunteered. Taking on this kind of service was scary for me, as I never saw myself as an "organized person." But it led to reviving the New York Share-A-Day, an annual event for about two hundred participants, which I chaired for two years in a row. I had to work with conflicting personalities and practice the Steps and Traditions (including dealing with a near fist fight at the event!).

After about thirteen years, having paid off all my debts but the student loans, I started to get harassing phone calls again. My Pressure Group agreed that it was time for me to work toward closing that final debt. I tried to negotiate with the collection agency to shave off the substantial interest it had accrued, but they wouldn't give in—and this really pissed me off. But my Pressure Relief Group put it in perspective for me: "Do you think you don't owe that money?" My disease still wanted something for nothing. Fourteen years after my first meeting, I paid what I owed and have had no unsecured debt to repay since. Thank God for a long, slow recovery. My goal in D.A. was never to repay my debts; repayment is the natural result of not debting one day at a time and taking care of myself by increasing my own prosperity and abundance. In order to do that, I had to have the patience and faith to put my creditors last—at the very bottom of my spending plan. That was a very scary concept to grasp early on, but it really works—in God's time, not mine.

After a few years in that executive position at my company, I found myself with a new vision: I wanted to write a blockbuster international course. I brought it up in my Pressure Relief Meeting but had no idea how I could make a shift from administration. After a few years, an opportunity came along that would allow me to co-author a flagship course for the company. When my boss told me I'd have to do it without a royalty (because I was a salaried employee), I turned it down. They agreed to give me a small royalty and I gave up my executive position, quickly moving from daily anxiety to creative work that brought me nothing but enjoyment. The course was published after about four and a half years and has been a great success. I do extensive international travel promoting it, participating in professional conferences, and providing training workshops. This last year, the course brought in almost $10 million for the company, greatly increasing my income. And the course still hasn't hit its peak.

About two years ago, it became clear it was time to replace my car. I could feel myself procrastinating and I had to get closer to the program to move ahead. We finally bought one last year (after my Higher Power hit me over the head a few times with the repair bills for the old one) and I was able to pay for it in full—something I never could have imagined earlier. And my son was accepted to a college that offered a small scholarship. For the past two years, I have paid the remaining $26,000 of his tuition without having to take out any loans.

Over the next year, I will be working toward revising the course I co-authored. As the company changed the terms of our agreement by not letting me write any longer on company time, I'm working with my Pressure Relief Group to negotiate a new royalty. I have reached a place of peace knowing that whether they agree to raise it or not, I will be writing as an independent author—not as an employee. So either way, I'll be fine. It's not about the money; it's about what I'm willing to do. And recently I've become aware of a new vision—to leave the company and have my own business as a writing and editorial house for publishers. I had always looked at D.A. business owners as strange aliens I would never understand, but suddenly I find myself thinking it's time to get me to a B.D.A. meeting.

Last year, I began a new level of service as a D.A. trustee. As usual, I face doubts about my ability to perform the service, but I try to show up and put one foot in front of the other. I also know that service always brings me to a new place in my recovery. After a year, I can still see how much I don't know. But I can also see how much I've learned and grown. And I know that this is only the beginning. One thing I'm certain of is that D.A. is my fellowship for life. I don't see myself reaching a place where I don't need the program. As a matter of fact, I sincerely believe that if I were to disconnect from D.A., the long slide would begin all over again. Every day, I am grateful for the miraculous gifts I've received by working this program one day at a time.

Originally published in the first edition of A Currency of Hope as "Busting out of Debtor's Prison"; updated and posted on the Debtors Anonymous website as "A 'Long, Slow' D.A. Recovery Brings Prosperity and Joy."

11

Less Is More

*D.A. gives her the tools to face her financial
situation honestly and responsibly.*

I grew up in a modest home where money was not highly valued, but financial responsibilities were taken seriously. My father was an alcoholic, but was not particularly frivolous with money. I think my mother resented the money that he spent on booze, but the negative financial effect of his alcoholism came more from how it limited his ability to earn rather than leading him to be profligate in his spending.

The alcoholism at home was extremely shameful to me, but I never discussed it with anyone in my family until I was in my twenties. It finally occurred to me that I might benefit from Al-Anon. I didn't take to it right away, but I continued to go to meetings and finally I made the first breakthrough that would eventually lead me to Debtors Anonymous—I discovered that I was actually an alcoholic myself, and started going to A.A. I knew I had a great deal of alcoholism on both sides of my family, but I thought it wouldn't be too hard. I was very surprised to find that it was really difficult for me to stay sober, especially for the first two years.

Eventually I became more comfortable with sobriety, and my money problems started to take a different form from the sort of slow-motion, chronic underearning I had experienced as an active alcoholic. I had worked in a creative field that I loved; unfortunately, it demanded a great deal of time and was very financially insecure. My husband and I had a young daughter now, so I reluctantly came to the conclusion that motherhood would not mix well with it.

I left that creative field and went into business with a partner in a field that I thought might be more lucrative, and in which I had natural talent—computer programming. Our business expanded quickly. We struggled for a while, but then suddenly our earning took off. Within two years, I was able to pay off all my credit card debt—probably about $20,000 worth—and my partner and I bought comfortable homes. That may have been the most dangerous thing for me, because I concluded that debt was no problem—I'd already beat it, hadn't I?

Ironically, I believe that my recovery from alcoholism had unleashed a dangerous character defect that didn't cause me much trouble when I was still drinking, but eventually led me to uncontrolled debting. It was my grandiose assumption that money was not really worthy of my concern. When I was still drinking, living small, and not making decisions about large amounts of money, I couldn't do much damage. But now that there were important decisions to be made, I needed my wits about me. Unfortunately, getting sober did not cause me to think clearly about everything right away. I persisted in a kind of magical thinking—that as long as I continued to focus on my dreams, then the universe would cooperate. Vagueness was a perfect "substance" for me to use to avoid experiencing reality.

As quickly as our business rose, it started to fall. We had become dependent on a single large client, and that business was now going away. Rather than liquidating the business, closing it in an orderly way, and preserving some of our assets, we continued to pour all the money we had earned back into it. When that ran out, we used our own money. All the while, we were slowly slipping into deep debt on a credit line that a bank had eagerly given us in our heyday.

The rise and fall happened so fast. By the time I was five years sober, my partner and I had more than $600,000 in debt. I continued to share my troubles in Alcoholics Anonymous, and it was a fellow member there who urged me to try D.A.

I started to keep track of all my spending. I was delighted to do this because it was one of the few things I seemed to have control over. I dove into the program, going to many meetings and getting active. My business partner also joined the program for a while, and somehow we were able to stop debting, both personally and in our business. It lasted for nine months, and then we had a business setback. We fell back into a debting pattern to keep the business going, and I fell into an eighteen-month relapse, continuing to get into more debt.

Because much of my debt was tied up with my business partner, I couldn't see how I could make my own decisions. Also, although my business failure had made my family less secure, I secretly blamed my husband, who had never earned much and was not likely to earn more. Finally, when I was telling a D.A. friend that all my problems were really Al-Anon problems, he said, "If you had an A.A. sponsee who told you she would stop drinking when she was able to straighten out her marriage, what would you say?" That stopped me cold and pushed me into making a serious commitment to stop debting one day at a time, no matter what.

Somehow, that commitment allowed me to leave that business within the next year and get a pleasant "recovery job" that paid me enough to meet the needs of my family. My relationships with my husband and my daughter improved immensely. I gradually began to pay down my debt and began saving for my retirement.

Today, thirteen years later, I have plenty of challenges, yet I really do have a life beyond my wildest dreams. I have a wonderful, challenging and responsible position in a business area that requires tremendous creativity—communications and marketing. I've paid off more than $50,000 in debt. I have resources to provide my family with appropriate medical care. I paid for my daughter's tuition to a private college without incurring debt. I was able to care for my mother during her final years, manage her money responsibly, and eventually manage her estate after she died. I've been able to travel to visit people who are important to me. And my husband and I are saving for a comfortable retirement, which I'll be able to take while we're still young and healthy enough to enjoy it.

D.A. has given me the tools to face my financial situation honestly and responsibly, yet in a balanced way. On the way, I'm having a terrific time. I can hold on to my good ideals and replace the mistaken ones. In a funny way, I was sort of right that money isn't that important. I have much greater blessings in my life than money, yet giving the right sort of attention to the material realities of my life has let me enjoy the very best that life has to offer. D.A. has taught me to recognize when less really is more.

Originally posted on the Debtors Anonymous website as "A Debtor Finds a New Life, in Which Less Really Is More."

$\sim$

God Is My Business Partner

A businesswoman finds a working partnership with her Higher Power.

I have always been a businesswoman, even as a small child. I guess you could say I think like a businessperson. My first business venture began when I was twenty-one and newly married. My (then) husband was from an entrepreneurial family and so was destined to have a business of his own. I more or less went along for the ride.

What a ride it was! We knew very little about running a business. We were young and had no money in savings. We borrowed money from a family member (which is another story). What we did have was a lot of discipline, passion, commitment, perseverance, and time. Unfortunately, that wasn't enough. The business failed within two years. For many years I considered myself a failure. Thankfully, one day my dad said, "You didn't fail, the business did."

That was B.D.A. Lesson No. 1: We surrendered to the idea that we are neither our business nor our debts. I thought I was the business. I was relieved that the business failed so I didn't have to do it anymore. Where was God during that two-year period? Nowhere to be found.

I moved on to Business No. 2. I started that business while finishing up with Business No. 1. I was proving to be a diligent workaholic, as many business owners are. I was twenty-three years old and full of wounds associated with "not being enough." Through this business, which I stayed involved with for another two to three years, I performed for others in order to seek the approval of others. It certainly satisfied that goal, but again God was nowhere to be found. About this time, I fortuitously entered Twelve-Step recovery and began to allow God into some areas of my life, but not business. In a few years I was completely burnt out, hated the business, and was in the middle of a divorce.

Enter Business No. 3, a business built purely on survival. I had very little money, a rocky self-esteem, and no direction. I was just trying to get by. Since I was in the beginning of my recovery I devoted a lot of time to personal growth. This was great for me, but not so great for building a business. Where was God? Nowhere near me with this struggling business. It failed shortly afterwards.

I began my D.A. recovery in 1988. I got solvent quickly and fell in love with Debtors Anonymous. A few years passed. I remarried, to a man who had a strong work ethic but little business background. Although I hadn't been involved in a successful business, I was growing as a businessperson. The two of us made a great team and built Business No. 4, a successful business. There was a D.A. meeting in my area with an emphasis on business ownership that I began attending. I slowly began to allow God into my business. We had this business for six years before we sold it for a profit. It seemed to me to be a miracle. Looking back, I see clearly that I was letting God into this area of my life.

My husband and I took jobs and began to build personal wealth. I applied the D.A. suggestions and principles and have remained solvent ever since. We owned a rental property, which was Business No. 5, and I began a Business No. 6 on the side. Although I was personally working diligently in D.A., I reverted to a state where God was nowhere to be found in these businesses. Both of them proved to be unsuccessful externally. Internally, I viewed them as learning experiences and moved on.

About three years ago my husband started Business No. 7. I wanted nothing to do with it, declaring that I'd "been there, done that." It was about a year before I felt called to join in the venture. When I got involved I knew I was going to need all the help I could get. It is a large company with shareholders, many independent contractors, and was growing rapidly. I felt overwhelmed. I joined with a fellow D.A. member who was starting his first business, and began a Business Debtors Anonymous group in our area. God was definitely with me!

With Business No. 7, I have considered God my Business Partner. With this focus, business has taken on a whole new meaning. I surrendered to God's will with my role being a participant in the business. The first thing that happened once I claimed God as my Business Partner is that a contract with God came through during my writing time. It states essentially what I am willing to provide, and that God will give me the power to carry out my part.

In B.D.A. I have learned to put myself, my relationship with God, and my family all before my business. Often I have referred to the "Additional Tools for Business Debtors Anonymous" list of twelve suggestions that are guidelines for recovery. When I first began B.D.A., I had only completed three of the twelve, and I was very discouraged. I had no choice but to work through all twelve. I needed help, so I got to work. A year later I can say that all twelve are integrated into the business. It was a triumph to go to my home group to celebrate my success.

In B.D.A. I am reminded by the "How Does One Know if He/She Might Be Compulsively Debting in Business?" list what's important NOT to do in building a prosperous, debt-free, and solvent business. There are fourteen behaviors noted that eventually lead to compulsive debting in business. I am heading for problems if I don't heed any of these warning signs. In B.D.A. I am reminded that "as grateful as we are for these tools for business owners and the other tools of D.A., we have found that it is only through working the Twelve Steps of Debtors Anonymous that lasting solvency, recovery, and serenity may be obtained for our businesses and ourselves" (Business Debtors Anonymous pamphlet).

The most important thing I have learned in B.D.A. is that God has been with me in all of the businesses. It is I who have not been open and receptive to His partnership. I know today that they are God's businesses, and that I am a steward of the gifts and talents that have been given to me by Him. One day at a time I can show up to the business knowing that God is with me every step of the way. When I get completely off track I have the Twelve Steps of D.A. that will assist me in coming back into alignment with God's will for me and the business. Anyone who owns a business and is lucky enough to find B.D.A. is truly blessed. Today, I am grateful to call God my Business Partner!

I still occasionally struggle with feeling overwhelmed by the many roles I play in the business. I still resist God's calling to be a steward of my gifts and talents through the business. I am learning to accept the success that I deserve. I still feel angry when it's not easy, and I still want to quit about once a month.

Even with all the "stuff" that goes with business ownership, I know deep down I was born to be a businesswoman. It is when I step into this role with God as my Business Partner that I can clearly see His will and accept His power in carrying it out. B.D.A. is my reminder that there is enough time, love, and money for me to be the best businesswoman I can, one day at a time. Today when I ask, "Where's God?" the answer is: God is walking with me, guiding me, every step of the way.

Originally posted on the Debtors Anonymous website as "A Businesswoman Finds a Working Partnership with God."

13

~

A Focus on the Basics

Working the D.A. program pays big dividends toward this debtor's recovery.

I joined Debtors Anonymous on February 15, 1987, in Palo Alto, California. I found D.A. in the phone book, called, asked for help and literature, and a member sent it to me.

I was in debt and could not get out of debt no matter how hard I tried. I could not keep my checkbook balance above a few dollars—often less; had credit card and college loan debts; and had mortgaged my car to pay bills; then I had that payment to make, too!

I was working below my education level at a job I hated that didn't pay enough. The little extra income I did make from working at another job a few hours a week that was at my education level was so far away geographically that I barely broke even after all that time on the road. I was sober and clean from drugs since January 15, 1977, and from alcohol since June 17, 1979, and regularly participated in A.A. and still do. But I could not get the money thing, nor get out of debt. I needed extra help.

From the first meeting I attended I loved D.A. These people were dressed nice, their hair was kept nice, they had jobs, were positive, were working the D.A. program, and paying off their debts. They too had been where I was, so they understood. I was welcomed. It felt good and I felt relieved. I did what they told me to do—attended meetings, kept daily records of my income and expenses, cut up my credit cards, closed accounts, had Pressure Relief Meetings for myself, was on Pressure Relief Groups for others, and started paying off my debts. It worked.

I went through withdrawal at first from not debting. It was a weird feeling, almost like a drug withdrawal. It passed. Where once money looked like a green piece of paper that had no weight, substance or meaning, it began to have value. I lost my first two Ideal Income Spending Plans: I think it was sabotage, as when I did them I found areas I had deprived myself and saw just how much I had been out of touch with hopes, dreams, my real feelings, and my own life.

I used the Twelve Steps to help me deal with those feelings. The third Ideal Plan I was able to bring to a Pressure Relief Meeting. I sweated so badly I had to remove a shirt and sit there in my tee shirt! My PRG people helped and supported me. We also used a guide, which I liked because it is a methodology format to follow that kept us focused. It worked.

I took my year and a half's experience in D.A. in Palo Alto with me when I moved back to the Midwest to see my ailing grandmother. There were no meetings, so I started one. I kept in touch by phone with friends in California and kept on working the program. I got out of debt on October 15, 1989, that way. D.A. helped me take a spiritual pilgrimage to Garabandal, Spain, buy a vehicle, visit the grandmother whom I cherished, get a degree in art painting, and build a prudent reserve. When I was ready to move on to the Southwest, I had the money to do so.

I've been in the Southwest since 1991 and still do the D.A. Tools of daily record keeping, including projected income and spending plans, adding to my prudent reserve so I have it to use when I need it, and I recently finished a six-month literature service position. I sponsor a man, also. I talk confidentially to my priest and work the Steps with him. And thanks to D.A. I bought my own mobile home, art studio, and truck. I paid cash and have no mortgage, which was one of my goals. I do artwork, get paid for it, and teach part time.

I am still in process and keep on repeating the basics to maintain and grow. Working the Twelve Steps specifically with a D.A. focus has created a shift inside me that I just could not seem to find in Alcoholics Anonymous, even though I love A.A. and have worked it faithfully for thirty years. I guess there was something in my mind that still needed a psychic change and a

Power I could trust with my whole life, including money, work, spending, time, and a real deep healing around pain and relationships. It is getting better. I am growing closer to being my real self and have so much today, free of so much baggage—resentments, fears, old ideas, and pain. I still use the Steps and Tools to live daily life, mature, and feel more of a sense of belonging, relaxation, and peace, knowing that I do have a Higher Power that hears and cares for me.

There is a sense of stability now, and willingness on my part to trust this Higher Power. This is a big step from being a kid who had nothing, not even hot or cold running water in the house on the farm, and no phone until I was nine. Due to very severe childhood and adolescent abuse, I thought God was deaf and did not care, so I gave up on God at age nine. It has been a very slow, piece-by-piece process to get to trust a Higher Power that I now know actually hears me and does care. I see evidences of it in my personal life. Daily I practice letting go to this Power, talking with it and trying to work with it better.

I don't understand even half of what and why things are the way they are on the planet, but I personally have a part to play and I am committed to playing my part. It helps a great deal to have the Twelve Steps, Tools, meetings, and service work. We are very lucky to have these things. We have a way out, a way that provides us with a sure anchor, a sure method for dealing with our fears, resentments, confusions, successes, numbers, actions; a way out in which there is a program to empower us to be who each of us really is, and to deal with pain and suffering in the world. I feel more peaceful, optimistic, and relaxed than I ever have.

It feels good to have a nice home and not be homeless. It feels good to have money in the bank, some nice clothes, do my artwork painting guardian angels for people and pets, and actually get paid for it. It feels good to be of service. It feels really good and it's a big relief to have a Higher Power to ask, "Hey, what do I do next? You want me to do what? How do I do this? What is my business? I need more courage than fear to do my part here!"

Thanks to D.A. and my Higher Power, I am no longer alone. I never was.

Originally published in the 2008 second-quarter issue of *Ways & Means* as "A Focus on the Basics Brings Him Twenty-one Years of D.A. Growth and Healing."

14

A Storybook Credit Card Debtor

*His mother gave him his first credit card and
his first D.A. meeting. He did the rest.*

I've often thought that the events that brought me to D.A. were not gory
enough. After I got to the program, I heard people talk about being arrested, garnishment, repossessions, and judgments from credit card companies.
My circumstances seemed to pale in comparison to those stories. Somehow
I'm sure now that the degree of gore is irrelevant. What is relevant is whatever
got you to D.A. and keeps you coming back.

I was a storybook credit card debtor. My mother gave me my first credit
card shortly before I went off to college. Even though the card was on her account, I started charging recklessly. I loathed paying her for things I charged.
After college, I began accumulating department store credit cards and major
credit cards of my own. I got a great job, a nice apartment, new friends, and
yet, I was miserable. Earlier that year, I had revealed my sexual orientation to
my mother. We went through a very difficult time exchanging hateful com-
ments and accusations. By the time graduation rolled around, I had put my
sexuality on the back burner, but the pot was slowly coming to a boil.

That summer the pot boiled over. My father died suddenly, which sent me
into a near-catatonic state. A few days after the funeral, my mother, frustrated
by the silence, told me she was glad my father never knew of my homosexual-
ity. She said that he never would have been able to deal with it, and if he had

not died of a heart attack, my being gay would have killed him for sure. The saddest thing of all is that I believed her.

Strangely enough (although looking back maybe it wasn't so strange), that month was the first time I received a credit card bill of my own. After all those years of never seeing the actual bill from my mother's account, I discovered that credit card companies did not, in fact, require you to pay in full, as my mother had. The words "minimum payment" became music to my ears and a new way of life.

Four years later, when I realized I could no longer meet even minimum payments on my credit cards, I panicked. It took effort to make sure my mother never knew of my difficulties. I got a second job to help catch up on my bills. I stopped going out completely. I figured I was safe if I stayed home locked in my apartment, far from the lure of using my credit cards for clothes that didn't fit, gifts for people, or things I didn't need. I figured it was a kind of punishment for all the debting I had done. I sidestepped all conversations about money, and I didn't answer the phone before 9:00 p.m. I threw all my unopened bills into a shopping bag. I was sure I could clean up my mess, or better yet, I would wake up one day and the mess would be gone.

Months later I was awakened by my mother calling to tell me that one of my creditors had called her to collect money, because I had not responded to their calls or correspondence. I was devastated. I felt ashamed. Now I had my mother on my back, which scared me more than any creditor could. More humiliation followed when, at my mother's insistence, I flew home, carrying my shopping bag full of unopened bills, to go to our local town bank so she could co-sign a loan to pay off my debts. I was mortified when my mother said to the bank office, "If he's even one day late on the payment, call me. Don't even bother calling him."

I handed over eighteen credit cards to my mother and kept one for emergencies (ha!). I told my mother it was in her best interest to let me keep one major credit card to charge airline flights. In the event of my death, she would be the beneficiary of $300,000 from a life insurance policy I got when I charged flights. With the money from the loan my mother co-signed, all my creditors were paid off. Now I had only one payment to make to the bank. I felt naked. Within a month, I had called six of my old creditors to get new cards. For the next year and a half, I rode the debting roller coaster. All I had to do was make sure I paid the bank on time. My other six creditors didn't have my mother's address or phone number, so I was safe. Soon enough, I was clothed with guilt again. Creditors were calling me at work. I was placed in collections and written off by a few. All my credit cards were at or near their maximum. I used to sit up at night at my kitchen table smoking cigarettes and fantasizing about winning the lottery. I used to try to figure out who I would pay off first.

When the phone company shut me off for nonpayment, I had to go to the business office to pay the bill. I stood in line in my suit, crisply starched shirt, and my perfectly scrubbed exterior and listened to other unfortunate people explain why they could not pay their bills. I couldn't believe they could make up such lies. When the service representative told me they would turn my service back on without a security deposit because I had been such a good customer I was thrilled. I smugly replied that I was glad she noticed. I added, "Why, I could have put a child through college on what I've paid the phone company. At least I feel better that I didn't make up a story about why I couldn't pay like the other people here today." I was so proud of myself, I went to the nearest department store and charged something.

A few months later, I was finally cut off from writing checks at the grocery store. That had been my last salvation. The next day my mother called. The bank had finally called her, because I had been late on the loan payment for nine months in a row. Oddly enough, my mother didn't yell or scream or say anything nasty. She did tell me she wouldn't help me out this time. She asked me if I knew about Debtors Anonymous. I had seen a meeting notice in a community calendar for a D.A. meeting on Fridays for the past two years. Then she asked if I wanted to go to a meeting now, and I said yes. She said, "If you go to D.A., I'll leave you alone. I can't help you anymore, but I think D.A. can."

I wanted to hang up fast and race to that meeting, except it wasn't Friday! The magic words my mother said kept ringing in my ears: "If you go, I'll leave you alone." It was worth going just for that. For an instant, I was angry that she hadn't offered to pay off the loan, but from the very first minute I walked into D.A., I realized my mother had done me a favor by not bailing me out. In D.A. I heard the same stories with different sets of circumstances, some worse, some better, some about the same. I also heard people talking about their visions, and the steps they were taking to do things in abstinence. What I saw, however, was more important. I saw people at peace.

After a while, things began to get better. I heard fantastic slogans like "I am not my debt" and "I owe my creditors money, not my self-respect." I had regular Pressure Relief Groups, and I gave Pressure Relief Groups. I did the actions on my action plan. I did service in meetings, and eventually I managed the D.A. phone in our city. I was always stunned when people approached me after meetings and said, "You were the voice on the phone. You listened to me and didn't tell me I was stupid or bad that I had gotten into debt. My life is so much better since I got to D.A." I always thanked them and added, "That was God's voice on the phone, not mine."

When I did my first Fourth Step, my mother's name came up all over the place. I kept going back to read my favorite story in the A.A. "Big Book," "Doctor, Alcoholic, Addict." I loved reading over and over, "If you had my wife, you'd drink too." It was exactly how I felt about my mother. For years, I had told my friends, my family, and just about anyone who would listen how crazy my mother was. Who could blame me for being such a mess? When I was a teenager, my mother told me I'd probably grow up to be an alcoholic. I guess I showed her; I did everything else but drink!

What my first inventory revealed, and what nearly every inventory has revealed since then, is quite simple. The exact nature of my wrongs was not my mother, my dead father, my sister, my brother, my aunt, my uncle, my lovers, my friends, my bosses, my creditors, my sexuality, or anything else that was put in my path. It was me, and how I reacted. It was my inability and unwillingness to live a spiritual life—spiritual laziness.

I felt, after a year or two, that the compulsion to debt using credit cards and other forms of unsecured debt had been lifted. Now when I am afraid to look at my checkbook, hesitate to spend money in one of my categories, or don't total my numbers for a few months, I go back to the basics and the spiritual principles of the program. Working D.A. when there are no crises to manage is hard only when I try to do it alone.

I have often thought that years ago I must have a dug a deep hole and buried all my visions in that hole. Every charge, every bad check I wrote, every resentment I had toward someone else, and every gossipy word out of my mouth was like throwing a shovel of dirt on top of those visions. Working the

Steps and doing a Fourth Step is like digging out of the hole one shovelful at a time. Sometimes the dirt falls back into the hole, and I have to dig out again. Sometimes the visions are buried so deeply that I have to jump into the hole to carry them out gently with my hands. I think sharing this process with other people who are doing the same thing is what makes it work.

One of the visions that is materializing for me is figure skating. I started skating when I was eight. I was the only boy in our town who did figure skating, so I was harassed a lot. I skated in the local ice shows, and I eventually skated a solo and did some ice dancing. When I was seventeen, I stopped skating. To continue would have required money and time. For fifteen years I told people that I stopped because my mother wouldn't pay the money. I now know that was a lie. I stopped because I was scared. In fact, I never even asked my mother for the money. I just assumed her answer would be no.

Over the years I skated occasionally, but never attempted a jump, spin or dance pattern. Last year I tired of skating around the rink without doing anything. I realized with the help of my program that if I didn't do something, I would die spiritually. I started lessons again and bought a pair of expensive skates. I had skating as a category in my spending plan. I go to skating events and watch them on TV, all extremely painful for me before D.A. I'm learning dance patterns and have again started to jump and spin. Sometimes I am still afraid to fall or I feel intimidated by other skaters. I have a spiritual strength I didn't have when I was seventeen.

As my visions unfold, I have held onto one thought—that visions are not about my job, my apartment, my car, vacations, my new relationship with my mother, or even figure skating. Visions for me are about balance, balance with God and the world around me. In D.A., I've attained what I consider material prosperity as well as great spiritual and emotional prosperity. I used to say in D.A. meetings that my car made my heart sing or skating made my heart sing. Now I feel that being balanced is what really makes my heart sing.

Originally published in the first edition of *A Currency of Hope*.

15

Higher Power Is Driving

She wanted somebody else to take care of her. She knew she couldn't do it herself.

The story of my life in D.A. is one that is still unfolding. I have only begun to identify the ways I am changing now: the illumination, the burdens made lighter, paths made clearer. But I am a willing participant in this discovery process.

First and foremost, the tenth and eleventh Signposts on the Road to Becoming a Compulsive Debtor have been true for me since childhood: First, I believed that someone else would take care of me, so I wouldn't have to. I believed I was not capable of taking care of myself. Throughout my eight years of college, I never gave a thought to what my earning capability would be, nor did I ever speak to anyone about a career path. I was and am now an artist, and that is all I ever wanted to be. When a lucrative and viable career in commercial art came my way, I frustrated hopeful employers with my lack of ambition, squandering opportunities that others would have treasured. I was emboldened to leave the field altogether when I met the man who would become my husband. He struck me as a strong candidate for rescuer and caretaker of me and my stray life, despite the fact that he was broke and rootless himself, a stray seeking some sort of refuge.

Through the years we've been married, we have racked up around $25,000 of debts on eleven credit cards. We've lived penniless and homeless, bought and lost a home in foreclosure, bought another home, and gone through twenty-six automobiles, to name a few of our trials and inanities. I now see my use of credit cards was an act of aggression toward my husband, punishing him for not taking care of me. Never once in my debting days did I give a thought to paying the money back.

My husband's debting was motivated by his own issues, which I have learned are not for me to judge or analyze. I am responsible for my own lot in life, and the good and bad of it has come to me because of who I am. I would love to blame my husband for our debt problems, but fortunately now understand the relationship between taking responsibility and accepting my life so I can make the most of my gifts.

My first discovery in D.A. was my belief that if I ignored my problems they would cease to exist. I came into the program at a time when I had decided to take the family finances back into my own hands. In desperation my husband had been throwing the unopened bills into a cardboard box. The job of sorting and clarifying our debts was enormous. The job of contacting each creditor was even bigger, and it was extremely emotional and exhausting. But the payoff in D.A. was regaining my dignity as I faced reality, when the cloud of vagueness began to fade away.

I did my initial work with the help of program calls and a few meetings. Then, I thought I had everything under control and quit D.A. I thought my involvement in another Twelve-Step program would address any issues that could come up. Six months later I found myself even more desperate and confused, and I was finally graced with the willingness to make D.A. a living part of my life.

Since that time, I have discovered a fellowship of loving, accepting support and help available in D.A. through meetings, personal contacts, sponsors, Pressure Relief Groups, and phone calls to members. I never cease to be amazed by the spirit of service that is alive in this program. It truly seems to be the case that members get as much out of helping others as they do out of being helped.

For me, the most important part of the program is learning to recognize my Higher Power's presence in my life, and coming to believe I am taken care of, with all my needs met; that I will not be abandoned; that I can dispense with the homelessness contingency fantasies. It is not my husband or my father who is my provider. All abundance, goodness, and wealth are from God.

Here is an example of God's presence in my life today: My ca
apart, and we don't have the money to repair them, a familiar situatic
prayed for a car and wondered how long I could go on like this. My n.
offered to lend me her car while she is away, which is great. Today I got a call
from a friend who shared the good news that she'd just taken a temporary job
out of state, but she needs to do something with her car while she is gone.
Not only can we help one another, but she just happens to leave on the day
my mother returns!

Today I'm grateful to be alive. I accept my husband and myself as children
of God. I am grateful for the trials I've had to face, for they have shaped and
strengthened me. I am willing to do whatever my Higher Power places before
me, whether that means speaking up honestly to my loved ones about difficult
issues, getting a job, taking a rest, or reaching out for help. Today is a beautiful
day, and I have everything I need.

Originally published in the first edition of *A Currency of Hope.*

16

Watching a Fellowship Grow in the U.K.

She learns to detach from her debts and build her faith in a spiritual D.A. program.

I was standing outside a church door with a few other members of Alcoholics Anonymous in the rain, waiting for the keyholder to arrive. I was aware that I was talking when a young woman turned on me and almost shouted, "Why don't you just get a job?"

I had the sort of shock that goes directly to the centre of my being. In that moment I felt the crash inside myself between what she said and the impossibility of me following through. Maybe I had been complaining a bit too much, but if she had been me she would have a lot to moan about too.

I was a deeply unemployed makeup artist. I had loads of debt, but was not sure how much. That day I had gotten into trouble with the bicycle shop as I could not pay for a puncture repair. I rang Mary in A.A. and she talked about Debtors Anonymous. I got very annoyed. After all, I was not one of those losers! I was just having a bit of bad luck. The government had created a massive downturn in 1989 that had caused me to be in such a mess by 1991.

There were too many makeup artists and I was vastly unappreciated. I had been taken advantage of over a workshop I had intended to do something interesting with, not sure what, but I had sublet it, and the tenant had not paid

anything for three years. The incredibly cheap rent in my flat w₍
and a half years in arrears, but the landlord had sent me an unclear s₍
I had no intention of paying until he made it clear. I had bought a hou₍
the Coast on a whim in 1988 and had given it back to the bank in 1990. It
was now full of addicts and managed by the only agent notorious for taking landlords' rents, folding her company, and then starting again. I worked
so hard I was exhausted—getting work, saving money, getting food left over
from the street market, buying clothes from the charity shops. But I was not
a debtor, no way!

Mary sat on the phone and listened. I told her too much detail of why it
was not my fault. I was sure I had convinced her. She gently suggested that
I get hold of a book on debting, write down everything I spent in all its tiny
detail, and come to a meeting of D.A. After six weeks of keeping my figures I
could call a Pressure Relief Group. This was made up of two people in D.A.
who would help take the pressure off me wherever it fell.

There was only one D.A. meeting at that time outside the United States,
and that was on a Monday night in central London. I waited for six weeks,
writing down everything I spent; then I let D.A. be graced with my presence.
I was prepared to show these losers I was not a debtor, but a poor girl who had
been dealt the most terrible of hands. I sat in the meeting not listening to the
other five people. I told everyone I was a great makeup artist and that they
were lucky to know me. I vaguely recognized another lady. A long while later
she told me she had spent a whole afternoon with me talking about D.A. I had
a complete blackout about that meeting.

At the end of the meeting I accosted the secretary and demanded he give
me a Pressure Relief Meeting. He looked a bit annoyed and suggested six
in the morning that Friday. I never got out of bed before eleven, but out of
bravado I agreed and then told Mary what I had arranged. Unbeknownst to
me she was in love with the secretary and also unbeknownst to me she was
still debting heavily. It was June 10, 1991. So that Friday morning in central
London we met up with my figures of everything I had spent over the last
six weeks—every cup of tea, every newspaper, and me with a seriously self-
righteous attitude.

The two looked at my figures and gently pointed out that I was some
£20,000 in debt, but that all I needed to stop debting was to earn £94.70. I

could not believe it. I was desperately ashamed and completely elated at the same time. I did not have to pay the debt back first; I just had to earn that tiny amount of money and worry about the debt later. They explained that unsecured debt was anything that I borrowed where nothing happened if I did not give it back. So from a pencil to cash, if I did not exchange it for something of the same value it was a debt.

I left the Pressure Relief Meeting on a high. London was still on its way to work and I was going home to think about how I could get some money. I received a phone call from someone who was about to take some exams. "Can you look after my old lady with Alzheimer's for the next four weeks? She does not need much. You give her a suppository before lunch and then take her her tray of lunch, made up from the night before, and make sure she does not fall over," she said.

"I am really busy and I don't like ill people," I said. "You finish at 4:00 p.m. and every day her daughter gives you £75 in cash," she begged. I jumped. In one day I could make most of the amount I needed to stop debting one day at a time. I took the job.

In the afternoon another friend, a co-debtor, rang to have the weekly moan about money. I told her I had had a revelation and that I only needed to earn £94.70 to stop debting. She was as shocked as I was. She said someone she knew needed help "looking things up." She gave me the number, I rang it, and the voice at the other end asked me to come into the office at 5:00 p.m. that day with my bank details, which I did. She was in a turmoil of papers and phones so I did not find out what the job was. She did ask me whether I was a member of the British Library. I wasn't, but said I was and joined on Saturday. By Monday I had worked for the old lady, been to the Library where I had asked the staff there to help answer the questions, and then I went to the D.A. meeting.

Even I had to agree there was something going in way beyond my comprehension. I paid off some of my cash debts within the first few weeks, the old lady went into a care home, and I got as much work as I wanted at the Library. A few months later I learned I was working for a huge art publication, and I had consistently done well in the audits of the other researchers. The editor asked me what my doctorate had been in! I explained I had failed all my exams and had no degree at all. She looked shocked and said she was only supposed to employ postgraduates at the very least, but as I had done so well she would keep quiet about it if I did. That first Friday she had been too chaotic to ask, so I did not have to lie.

I have gone into some detail about my first week all those years ago to show that despite a stinking attitude, poor recovery around me, and no literature except a non-Conference-approved book, my life was changed despite myself, just by sharing with other debtors. We all shared with one another every Monday and gradually the Fellowship grew. I started a number of meetings, gave PRGs, and watched as literature finally arrived from America.

We evolved Spending Plans before computers were commonplace, using accountancy books. I used a prepaid phone card and jumped into phone boxes all the time to ask the smallest thing about my finances from any other D.A. member. Using the awareness tool, I started to read the financial sections of the paper, understanding very little.

I went to court over some of my debts and made arrangements to pay them off, all the time talking and talking to other D.A. members, sometimes for hours until they were begging to get off the phone. I became consumed by the program in a positive way. I was hungry for recovery! Then about three years in, I got a massive bill of £33,500 for the house I had given back. This meant my total debt when I came in was £56,500. By now though, I had faith that D.A. would help me out. I had learned to detach from my debt.

There was a legal process going through the courts arguing that negative equity did not have to be paid off, so I decided to enter into negotiation. It took five years, but on March 28, 1997, I paid off the last of my debt. Since then I have been totally free of any unsecured debt. I got a sponsor in 1996 and worked the Steps every Tuesday at 6:00 p.m. for an hour. After a while my sponsor found out what I was earning and, deeply shocked, said I was massively underearning. I nearly hit him, but sat there just fuming. I still acted like a victim. A visitor from New York said he would help me start a Business Owners Debtors Anonymous meeting. He brought some literature and that was the last I saw of him, but I waited, and after about three months I had two others committed to the meeting.

I did a very basic computer course. That December a friend gave me her boyfriend's number, saying he made good money out of computing. I had recently been diagnosed as dyslexic and could not see how I was going to change from being an underearner, still a victim. I made the call and he suggested I go into loads of employment agencies and do their tests until I started to pass them, then to come back to him. I did as I was told; I was learning slowly to do what I was told. I ended up working at night in a bank five nights a week and my income had jumped from £12,000 a year to £50,000.

I could not spend it and had just bought my flat at a discount. I got shouted at and bullied. I did not understand the banking world; I did not like my team. I kept at it. I learned how to get the computer to tell me what my dyslexia could not. I got sacked. I got another job and got sacked, and this continued. I knew why I was not up to the job but I kept quiet and did the best I could, and went to lots of meetings in the evening. I worked the Steps on my being a victim, being dishonest, being a drama queen. I learned that as a debtor I wanted something for nothing and this is best counteracted by service. I took on sponsees and did more service. "Service makes me rich" is my mantra for newcomers.

My definition of rich means in all areas of my life. I joined Intergroup, and because of the graveyard hours shared a lot on debtors websites. I then made a commitment to have a convention for the next ten years. This year (2010) is the tenth, and it has been a thrill to see it growing and growing. Small groups all over Europe send people over to England, and we talk to each other, growing D.A.

Things changed in London after September 11, 2001, and I got sacked again. I was sacked on the third of December and paid off the last of my mortgage on the fifth of December. I was debt-free. What was I going to do with my life? A friend suggested we go to India. After a Christmas and New Year on the beach there, I went to buy a carpet that had been on my wish list. As I was leaving the pool in the morning, an Englishwoman who had ignored us for the whole three weeks swam towards me. She told me not to bother getting out of her way as she was used to her own pool in Spain. I asked why she was here in India when she had a pool in Spain. "Tax exile, darling," she said.

A voice from somewhere came out of my mouth and said, "Tell me if I am being rude, but could you tell me how?" I promise I do not say these sorts of things. There followed a six-hour workshop on how to make money. She and her husband told me to write everything down, not to debt and keep my eyes and ears open. I had my Steps, I had my figures, I felt free to tell them what my assets and defects were both in character and finances. They told me story after story, always with the emphasis on having fun.

I came back to London and started a business buying and renting property. I am now a millionaire with no unsecured debt. I share my story to illustrate that at no point did I have a clue how things would turn out, and indeed I still don't. I have learned to do what the program tells me, and trust my HP has got fun and games for me ahead. I am still financially fearful at times, but I just recognize it as an old annoying friend. I work with others and recognize that confused, bewildered Princess who came in, so hopeless and angry.

I have moved from a flat to a four-bedroom house with a garden in central London. This week I have a tiny amount of cash to spend, but my refrigerator and car are full. My bills are paid and by Monday, all being in the plan, I will get another large rush of money, which I will carefully allocate according to my Spending Plan. I have had so much evidence that I am being looked after by whatever I think of as an HP. Whether I like it or not, I am getting rich and have been able to live without incurring any unsecured debt for many years now.

Originally posted on the Debtors Anonymous website as "In Britain, a Debtor Recovers—and Watches a Fellowship Grow."

17

My Surrender to D.A.

This debtor needed a lot of courage to face her creditors.
She found it with the help of her Pressure Relief Group.

When I first came to D.A. I was like a hamster or gerbil on a treadmill. I was racing faster and faster, working harder and harder to try to improve my situation, but it stayed the same no matter what I did. There was never enough money.

I paid all my bills late. I couldn't bring my credit card balances down. I owed $50,000 to my lawyer for a very nasty divorce, and I was constantly using my credit line. I alternated between spending as little as possible in an attempt to manage things and periodically spending when I couldn't stand the deprivation any longer. I overworked six or seven days a week, often evenings.

One year before I came to my first D.A. meeting, I had resolved to make more money. Surely that would be the answer to my financial problems. I was successful in increasing my income by a significant amount, but my situation remained exactly the same. I was baffled. I had tried everything I could think of; finally, I gave up. A friend had been telling me about D.A. for years, so I decided to give it a try.

What I heard at my first few meetings gave me hope. Since all my efforts had failed, I resolved to do whatever these D.A. people told me to do. I began by writing down everything I spent, getting rid of my credit cards, and paying my bills on time. After some initial shyness, I began talking to people after meetings, getting their phone numbers, and calling them.

I knew I needed to stop all forms of debting, that I needed to not incur any new unsecured debt. I was still involved in a custody battle with my ex-husband. I realized that continuing to use my lawyer's services would be debting, unless I paid her for those services promptly and in full. It was frightening to let go of her services in the middle of the custody case. As I shared this in a meeting, expressing all my fear and uncertainty, I cried. I said I needed a Pressure Relief Meeting. What an outpouring of support I received, including a woman who agreed to be on my Pressure Relief Group. I was so grateful.

Finding a man for my first Pressure Relief Group was harder. I asked men at every meeting I went to, but none were available. Finally, one Saturday morning, I called someone in D.A. who suggested I go to every meeting I could possibly get to—several each day if necessary—and ask every appropriate man. I took his advice and went to a meeting that afternoon. I heard a man with an inspiring qualification and promptly asked him to be my pressure man. Much to my surprise and joy, he said yes.

The love, support, and relief I felt from that first Pressure Relief Meeting was powerful. When they suggested that I take a moratorium on my debt payments, I was shocked. I left the meeting convinced that I would not have the courage to do such a thing. About a week later I decided to do what my Pressure Relief Group had suggested. I knew this meant giving up my lawyer. She would not represent me unless I continued to pay her $100 each week against my debt to her.

I contacted all of my creditors, both by phone and in writing. I kept a record of all calls and copies of all correspondence. I made lots of D.A. book-ending calls before and after contacting my creditors. I called my lawyer to let her know I would not be able to pay her for a while. She was furious and accused me of destroying her law practice. I was shaking, in a cold sweat. My heart was pounding, but because my pressure people had given me a script to follow and coached me, my voice was calm. I stuck to my script and didn't engage in any argument. I always assured all my creditors of my commitment to pay them the money I owed.

I began to take action toward finding affordable legal help. This was an act of faith. I made numerous phone calls and followed every lead. In the end I was offered free legal help from two sources. This was a D.A. miracle to me—just one of the many proofs I've experienced that I do have a Higher Power looking out for me. When I am committed to not debting, my Higher Power provides whatever I need.

Originally published in the first edition of *A Currency of Hope.*

⟆

18

An Entrepreneur Finds D.A.
and B.D.A. Recovery

*"I do the best and feel the happiest when I know in
my bones that my HP is my source."*

I didn't know there was such a thing as a compulsive disease called "debt-ing." I thought I was either bad or dumb. As I spiraled further and further down into debt, I tried to treat what I thought the problem was. To cure being dumb, I read books, hired consultants to tell me how to run my business, took classes, went to networking groups, and talked to other people in my field to try to learn how to work "smarter." To cure being bad, I did the Twelve Steps multiple times in other programs.

But until I found out what the problem was—compulsive debting—I couldn't apply any of the solutions people gave me. The best news I ever got was at my first Pressure Relief Meeting when one of the people said, "You're not bad or dumb. You're just insane." Thank God! I knew from previous experience where to go to be restored to sanity. Later, I heard someone say at a meeting who had come to D.A. from another Twelve-Step program that "the credits don't transfer." That explained it.

When I came to D.A. I was going to kill myself over my debts. I had no idea how much they were, nor exactly to whom I owed money; I just knew I owed a lot. I did know that I owed the IRS; they had placed a lien on my business because I had collected payroll tax money from my employees but hadn't paid this money to the IRS (this is called stealing). The state had also place a lien on the business for unpaid payroll AND sales tax (more stealing). I also wrote many bad checks. As part of my insanity, I wrote bad checks based on payments I knew were coming in. They always came, but later than I planned. So I incurred the humiliation of bouncing the check, and the financial pain of all the fees owed to the bank. Then I would cover the bad check one or two days after it bounced. I knew this was insane but I couldn't stop.

It took me five PRGs to finally get an accurate accounting of all the money I owed. It totaled a number in the mid six figures. I felt so ashamed of myself for incurring this much unsecured debt. The funny thing is, now when I do PRGs for people and they owe $20,000 or $75,000 or even $250,000 or more, I can tell them not to worry. I owed more than that. Today because of D.A., I am debt-free.

I don't know what happened to me exactly. I know ultimately it was the grace of God. I didn't do anything to merit such a dramatic turnaround in such a short time (it took two years and five months from the first day I walked into D.A. until all my debts were paid). I did work very hard in the D.A. and B.D.A. programs once I found them and realized my problem was compulsive debting, but lots of people do that, too.

A speaker came to talk to our group when I had been in the program for three months. I was still in terrible fear and pain. (Things got worse on the outside before they got better.) I knew I wasn't fit for much service to the program. I had no experience, strength, or hope. The speaker said, "Do what you can where you are." So that's where I started. I stacked a lot of chairs, smiled at a lot of newcomers, handed out literature, and picked up after the meetings ended.

I also took the Steps.

I knew from my other programs that our spiritual awakening comes from the Steps. Someone advised me to write my history with money to see my powerlessness and to help me take Step One. When I did that, I was surprised to find I had been insane about money a long time. My underlying belief was that if I had enough money, I didn't have to trust God.

When I first came into D.A., I stopped using credit cards. But I kept writing bad checks and paying bills late. I was underearning and didn't have the money to pay my bills. I was still writing bad checks when I started doing the Steps. I thought I should have stopped debting before I started the Steps; what happened was that doing the Steps helped me stop debting. Doing the Twelve Steps saved my life and gave me a foundation for my continued abstinence from incurring unsecured debt.

Part of the amends I owed were to my employees. I was no prize as a boss, but my greatest transgression was paying them late, and worse, occasionally bouncing their paychecks. I thought I would die of shame having to call them and ask how I could right this wrong. Paradoxically, the hardest part of these amends was the anticipation; actually making the amends was deeply freeing, and some of them are friends today.

On the surface, the money that paid all my debt and gave me a comfortable prudent reserve came from selling my business. People say to me "Yeah, but you had something to sell to get yourself out of debt." The funny thing is, when I first started working the program, having PRGs and doing the Steps, selling my business wasn't even a possibility. Possibilities and solutions appeared as I worked the program. When I did my first few PRGs, I figured it would take me twenty years to pay off all my debt. Somehow, my Higher Power managed it in less than three years.

I do the best and feel the happiest when I know in my bones that my HP is my source. Among all the other miracles this program keeps giving me, that one is the most profound, and the most life-changing. When I live in that certainty, anything can happen.

Originally posted on the Debtors Anonymous website as "An Entrepreneur Finds Recovery through D.A.'s Primary Purpose."

19

⌒⌒

Surrender and Service

On the road to recovery, this debtor passes milestones to true joy.

I got to D.A. "drowning and on fire" in the fall of 1995. As soon as I learned that Debtors Anonymous existed, I knew everything was OK. I knew the Twelve Steps, I knew they worked for me, and I knew I would do what I was told.

I couldn't wait to be told what works. I found a meeting about forty-five miles away, cut up my credit cards, and sent them back to the creditors. I found a man in my area with a little more experience than me and, along with my wife, we started a meeting in our town. I never used unsecured credit again. I worked the Steps, went to meetings, had Pressure Relief Groups, and began to live in the peace and the blessings of fiscal solvency. The trouble left what had been our financially "troubled" marriage. I began to experience the joy that recovery brings to life.

At my job my newfound clarity about money got me promoted to manager. I had what I wanted and rode that wave for another six years—always experiencing greater abundance than I had ever believed possible for me. I was slated to become the co-director of my company and eagerly waited my "final" promotion. I believed:

(a) The top was as high as I could go.
(b) My eyes could see the top.
(c) I was looking at it.

I was wrong about all three.

Throughout this period I had been keeping my numbers, intentionally working the Steps, and speaking to at least one D.A. member daily. On the morning of September 11, 2001, I made the decision to retire from my thirteen-year position. On that morning I understood there was probably more to life than my manager position, my salary, and the comfort of my familiar groove. I went home on February 15, 2002, and began creating my new life with a new goal: create and run companies. I didn't exactly know the details of what I wanted, but I knew the feeling of what I wanted. I had an emerging vision, but at that moment it was only a brighter spot in a foggy image.

About three weeks after I left my job, a similar corporation called and asked me to come and help solve some problems for them. I declined. I was retired. They called again and again. Nice people but they couldn't take a hint. I got tired of them calling and one day, to make them finally leave me alone, I told them "You can't afford me." The director on the phone simply asked "How much?" I gave an amount that I knew no one would ever pay me so she'd stop calling. To my shock, she immediately agreed to the fee. I hung up the phone and realized I had just created a consulting business.

I compiled a list of what I would do for them, completing that list in nine days and submitting my invoice. I was looking forward to going back to retirement. When I turned in the invoice the director said, "You can't leave!" Someone opened my mouth and replied, "I won't keep working for that amount," and we increased my fee by 50%. I was now charging what no one would ever pay me, plus 50%. I suddenly knew that The Rules I had always believed—about who I had become and what was possible—were shaky at best. Another company called. And another. And another. I had more money than ever flowing in, and I had the Tools I had learned in D.A. to use the money wisely and stay sane.

Twenty-five years earlier I had created a business that had become quite successful, but at that time I knew nothing about record keeping and nothing about solvency. When I owned that business I wanted to spend all the money, never go to work, and spend my days hanging out with friends. It's no surprise that I lost that business. It still exists today and it's been interesting to watch it grow—as a result of recovery, my feelings about my role in creating it have gone from painful to joyful that it still exists, and that it's now the dominant business in its field.

Now, in my new consulting business, I was succeeding. I knew about record keeping, keeping a prudent reserve, and staying solvent. Those were wonderful tools to bring to this business, but something was missing. I experienced a high level of fear of losing. I was filled with anxiety, trying to control things that were beyond my control.

In 2003, I began a service commitment that inspired me to go to as many meetings as possible in as many towns as possible. This was heaven to me. I loved our little rural home meeting, but I was suddenly exposed to more recovery, more inspiration, more ideas. I was receiving all the blessings that come from being of service. As a part of this service, I visited a Business Debtors Anonymous meeting with no idea of what it was. It took a while—three or four minutes—before I knew I was in the right place.

In B.D.A. I began to learn a new level of surrender. I could turn my will and my life over to my Higher Power, but it never occurred to me that my HP might have some business management guidance. A B.D.A. member shared an experience of being led to give up a good business for an unknown greater. At some level I understood him, and I tried what he described for finding Vision: I closed my eyes daily in meditation and wrote down whatever I saw. For three weeks I saw black. Every day at 3:30 I closed my eyes and saw black. Three weeks into this I realized I was watching a "movie" of me owning and running the type of business I was being hired to advise. I wrote it down but I thought it was wishful thinking. I was smart enough to know it couldn't happen, but it was a nice idea and I wrote it down because I didn't want to get in the habit of deciding which ideas that came in my meditations were the "good" ideas.

That was the fall of 2003. I was *given* my first of these businesses within two months, and took over that year. I was told I was chosen because of my experience and because I was solvent and financially stable. Somewhere along the line my reputation must have changed from desperate debtor, borrower, check bouncer. I know I was chosen because of all that I had received from D.A. and B.D.A., and because of my HP.

In August of 2004, while carrying out another D.A. service commitment, I received a phone call requesting I come to meet a board of directors I didn't know in a company I didn't know. They needed some help with a very small rural business that wasn't doing well. They couldn't afford me, so I decided to offer two free days of evaluation. We scheduled the meeting for two weeks later.

On the way to the meeting I was on the phone with a B.D.A. member. She gave me some advice that seemed important to my task at hand. What I got from her advice was to notice that I was praying to my Higher Power, but I wasn't paying any attention to the content of my prayer—I had no idea what I was asking for. I pulled off the road and began to write down my prayer. I wrote that I wanted to be of service to this agency and its clients. I wrote that I wanted increased prosperity and that maybe, someday, the board would give me this business. I arrived for the meeting the next morning, introduced myself and they gave me the business. Not "maybe, someday." They patiently waited while I gave my introductory spiel, and then asked, "Will you take over our business?"

I continued my daily vision meditation, eyes closed, pen and paper in my lap. I had stopped questioning the images that came to me—I simply wrote them down and wondered how in the world they were going to happen. (As time has passed I've realized that all of these visions are going to happen, but not "in the world.") Seventeen days before I took over that business I had a vision that I could now afford to buy some of these businesses, but, of course, no one would ever sell a business of this type. Two days later I received a phone call from a business owner with a chain of five similar businesses who wanted to retire. Three days before I opened the second business, I became a partner in that chain. From my original vision in 2003, I had seven businesses of a type that I knew was "impossible" to get. With the support of others in D.A. and B.D.A. I now run these businesses in financial solvency and debt-free. When I forget how incredible this is, my meetings remind me. When I try to take charge, my support system reminds me to turn it over.

Last year my wife and I had visions of being authors. We said we didn't know how to do that, but God said we did know how. Our first book is nearing the printing phase and should be in our hands in a few months. It's been an exciting process for us to sit at the keyboard and watch our fingers type and type. We're always amazed at what ends up on each page. I now have a new vision gaining clarity in my awareness. When the visions are big, they often come in little pieces that I seem to be able to grasp—little pieces on little pieces turning into big visions. I don't know how I'm going to create this vision, but I know it's coming. The wonderful news is that I've learned in recovery that causing it to manifest is not my job. Letting it manifest is my joy.

My certainty that none of this could happen was, fortunately, not as powerful as the Steps and my HP. I've come to realize that, at least in my life, those are the two most powerful forces that could exist—the Steps and God. I've learned to allow all answers to come in prayer. How much money should my businesses generate? I find the answer in prayer. How much should I pay my employees? I find the answer in prayer (God is always generous). How much money should I allow in my life? I find the answer in prayer. Where should I live? I find the answer in prayer. My life is a gift of surrender, inventory, prayers for personal and spiritual growth, listening to my Higher Power, honesty, more prayer, D.A. meetings, working the Steps, sponsoring, service, B.D.A. meetings, more sponsoring, working the Steps, meditation, and carrying the message.

I am a member of D.A. and B.D.A. and I find *recovery* there. I have no unsecured debt in my personal life and all of my businesses are debt-free. I'm recovering my awareness of my Higher Power. I'm recovering Joy. I'm recovering allowing myself to live a wonderful life. I'm recovering serenity. I'm recovering peace. Thank you, D.A.! Thank you, B.D.A.!

Originally posted on the Debtors Anonymous website as "Surrender and Service: Milestones on the Road to Joy."

20

⌒⌒

From Chaos to Clarity in Business

*This debtor discovers that not incurring new unsecured personal debt
or business debt leads to freedom from old debt.*

I got my first credit card shortly after I turned eighteen. Having grown up in
a family that could be classified as the "working poor," I saw credit as a way
to live the lifestyle that my parents never had the means to provide. I signed
up for every card I could get my hands on and began missing payments almost
immediately. It did not occur to me that the two minimum-wage jobs I had
were insufficient to cover my basic expenses and the rapidly increasing minimum monthly payments for my numerous credit cards. I think most people
would have taken this as a sign that they needed to change their spending
habits. Not me! In my opinion, as long as I looked good everything was cool.
I had a car, a motorcycle, a closet full of new clothes, and was trying to impress
my lady friends with expensive dinners and evenings out. Of course, the stacks
of unopened mail and unpaid bills continued to grow.

The first time I heard of Debtors Anonymous was while giving a co-
worker a ride to work. I had shared with this person that I had been attending
another Twelve-Step fellowship for a number of years, and she shared with me
that she was a member of D.A. I remember thinking how humiliating it must
be to have to go to a fellowship called Debtors Anonymous! Of course, in
retrospect, I was living mostly on borrowed money at that time and was more
than likely behind on my rent.

The motivation to go to my first D.A. meeting came from one of the guys who had helped me to get clean in another fellowship a few years earlier. I worked as a sales rep at his company and had just asked him for yet another commission advance to enable me to pay my rent. As he was writing the check for me, he looked at me with great sadness and told me he felt as though he was giving an alcoholic another drink. I respected this man's opinion of me. I also knew that he knew me well enough to be able to tell me what I didn't necessarily want to hear.

I reluctantly went to my first meeting. I did not want to be there. I sat in judgment of everyone in the group and decided that they were all way more screwed up than me. I left the meeting, got in my expensive car that I could not afford and drove to my apartment that I was facing eviction from. It's no wonder I felt superior to the "losers" at the meeting! The way I saw it, as long as I could continue to look good on the outside, my finances would eventually work themselves out.

It was a few years later that I began to attend D.A. regularly. By this time, any illusions I had of being able to "manage" my financial affairs had been shattered. My credit was ruined. I owed large amounts of money to all my closest friends, including the woman who would eventually become my wife. I had started a business that I used as a vehicle to create more debt in every way conceivable, including bouncing payroll checks to my employees. In addition to paying ridiculous amounts of interest on my unsecured debts, I was also paying thousands of dollars per year in overdraft and NSF fees. I was no longer able to keep up the "big-shot" appearance.

It took me almost two years of coming to D.A. on a regular basis to finally stop incurring new unsecured debt, one day at a time. I finally became willing to begin working the Steps in this program and began a series of Pressure Relief Meetings. My finances were such a tangled web of confusion that it wasn't until my third PRM that we were able to create my first income and spending plan. The vagueness of my spending seemed to be eclipsed only by my lack of clarity on how much money I actually earned, or didn't earn, from my various income sources.

For me, gaining clarity in my finances and getting some serenity as it related to my income required selling my business. I am not suggesting that that is the answer for everyone. But for me, I had so much emotional baggage wrapped up in this business it was the only way. Of course, I still had to work on me.

Since I have been working the D.A. program seriously, I have been able to pay off most of the unsecured debt I had accumulated, including the many thousands of dollars I had borrowed from my wife before we got married. My last remaining unsecured debt is to a friend and investor in the business I once had. I still owe her just under $15,000 and am making monthly payments in accordance with mutually agreed-upon terms. This is part of my amends to her for taking advantage of our friendship to meet my financial needs, even though I didn't see it that way at the time.

Not long ago I received a notice from a collection agency regarding a delinquent credit card account. This was rather surprising, considering I thought all my credit cards had been paid off for quite some time. It turns out that this was related to that first credit card I had received when I turned eighteen, over fifteen years ago! Having not seen this on my credit report in many years and having kept no records of it otherwise, I had completely forgotten about it. Even with the recovery I have in D.A., it was still difficult for me to take the action I knew I needed to take. As much as I hated to part with the money so many years later for a debt that seemed to be from another lifetime ago, it was clear to me after speaking with my sponsor and sharing about it at the group level that I needed to clean up this wreckage of my distant past. I negotiated a settlement with the collection agency and mailed them a check for the full amount of the settlement on the day that I told them I would. What a difference from my past experiences of trying to manipulate collection agencies to stall for more time!

I will soon be celebrating my fourth anniversary of not having incurred any new unsecured debt. I regularly attend one D.A. and one B.D.A. meeting per week, I am of service to D.A., I have been a part of countless Pressure Relief Groups, I have worked the Steps, I keep a current record of my income and expenses, and I also now keep my personal funds separate from my business finances. These actions help me to remain steadfast in my resolve not to incur any new, unsecured debt, one day at a time, no matter what!

I am grateful to D.A. and to my Higher Power for giving me the courage to face my shortcomings as they manifest themselves in the area of money.

Originally posted on the Debtors Anonymous website as "A Business Owner Finds His Way from Chaos to Clarity."

21

Debt Was Hazardous to My Health

She couldn't imagine life without credit cards.

Today I am wealthy and live prosperously. In just five years I have come from constant fear and contemplating bankruptcy to experiencing a sense of well-being and joy. It took a leap of faith to let go of my crushing dependency on credit and to trust that my security was dependent upon a Power greater than myself.

For me, it all started more than twenty-five years ago when I returned to my home state after my first two years in New York City. Until then, I worked only for myself, never considering using credit. When I got a job with a corporation, I borrowed $800 from the corporate credit union to buy a Chevrolet Custom Impala. The credit union painlessly withdrew monthly payments from my paycheck. When I sold the car a year later for $1,000, I paid off my loan in full. Little did I realize what long-term consequences a loan I could pay off would have. Little did I appreciate the freedom of a debt-free life.

The two categories of debt in D.A. are secured debt and unsecured debt. Secured debt has collateral, such as a house or car. D.A. addresses unsecured debt; that is, debt with nothing to back it up—debt with no collateral, such as credit card and personal loan debt. The car loan was the only secured debt I would have for the next fifteen years.

In the midst of the summer I turned twenty-six, I returned to New York with plans to start another business. I moved in with friends until I could earn some money for my own apartment. On a hot summer day, I detoured through a big department store to enjoy the air conditioning. A woman standing in the middle of a broad ground floor aisle stopped me and asked if I had the store's credit card. "Of course not," I replied. "Would you like one?" she asked. "Sure, why not," I said lightly. The air conditioning felt good, and I wanted to see the expression on her face when I told her my financial status. I was more than willing to give truthful answers to her personal questions: No job. No one supporting me. No house. No car. No apartment lease. No prior credit cards or bank loans. No private income. No assets. Nothing. Wait a minute, does a car loan from a corporate credit union count?

The address I gave her was in care of my friends—the clincher, I believed, to never getting that card. I didn't even want it. I didn't hope to get the plastic. I thought it was a big joke, and I was certain that I would not get the card.

The joke was on me.

That September I accepted a full-time job and soon used my grownup, permanent job status and my department store credit reference to get lots more credit cards. Later I used my salary increases to take out debt consolidation loans from time to time to clean up my credit act. Although I had sincere-yet-brief intentions of never borrowing on those cards again, the debt consolidation loans only freed up my cards and other lines of credit for yet another spree of debting.

I was not criminally motivated, and I borrowed and charged with every intention of repaying my creditors. I knew that I earned as much as the next person, and that on my credit applications, I honestly stated my income, expenses, other lines of credit, and whether or not I owned a house or car. I figured the people who gave me credit knew something I didn't; for example, how I would get the money in the future to pay for the things that I just couldn't live without—not so uncommon in these days of instant gratification.

However, as my debt escalated, my monthly payments to my creditors used up more and more of my cash. Within a few years, the only way I could buy clothes, go out to dinner, or pay for entertainment was to use my credit cards. Four years after I first applied for a credit card, I was using my credit cards to buy even groceries. At the time I earned about $15,000.

When I could admit and talk about my problem, a friend told me about a consumer credit counseling service. The next day I spoke with a counselor who took my $8,000 in bills, called my creditors, and negotiated a repayment plan with them all. I had only to send the service one monthly check, and they would send payments to my creditors. It was an almost painless way to solve the problem. Within a few years my debts were repaid, credit cards were mine to use again, and I was rewarded with bigger and better lines of credit. I had proven myself worthy of incurring a debt that was ridiculous in terms of my income, and then proven capable of repaying it. I had truly arrived as a good credit risk. I believed that as a seasoned credit card user, I had learned my lesson.

For six years, marriage intervened in my overspending habits. I set up our budget, because I was as acutely aware of my husband's extravagant spending pattern as I was blind to my own. Our money was shared. We both traveled extensively for work and had company expense accounts, relieving us of many of our day-to-day expenses. When we parted ways, he paid all our outstanding credit card bills. Once again I was left with a fist full of zero-balance credit cards.

For the next five years; I proceeded to incur over $25,000 of debt, including $2,200 in taxes. Fifteen years after I signed up for my department store credit card, I was working only three days a week and earned $36,000 annually, had an apartment lease, credit cards charged to the hilt, and two personal bank loans. I still had no house, no car, no one supporting me, no private income, no assets. I had begun a master's program by borrowing money from my father, but could not continue my education with loans. My personal credit limit was used up, and I earned too much to qualify for school loans. My problem, I thought, was that my father would not pay for my education. It did not occur to me that debting was making my life unmanageable.

My debt load went from 53% of my annual income to 70% of my annual income in about ten years. I was in complete denial about my problem with debt. Often it became necessary for me to borrow from one card to pay another or periodically refinance my personal loan, called "debt consolidation." I paid the minimum balance every month, my rent, and heard no warnings about where I was headed, except from my accountant. Appalled at the interest I was paying for years, my accountant had advised me to pay off my credit cards. I justified the interest I was paying, because I wrote it off on my income taxes. He mentioned that soon interest wouldn't be deductible, if I needed further motivation to get rid of these lines of credit. He would roll his eyes, and I would ask myself, "What would you expect from a penny-pinching accountant? No nickel and diming for me, thank you very much."

The first time I sensed that I might have a problem with debt was when I applied for yet another debt consolidation loan and was refused. Even though I paid my monthly bills like the good citizen I knew I was, there was no cash left even to buy tokens to get to work and back. Whatever formula "they" used to figure my capacity to borrow against those credit limits, I was no longer able to repay even the monthly minimum. Something didn't compute. When I calculated what my basic monthly expenses were, including my monthly minimums, I was shocked to realize that I could no longer live merely on a cash basis without being subsidized by a credit card. What was I thinking of? The answer is that I was not thinking, but that I was caught in the debtor's common symptom of "terminal vagueness." That glimmer of truth, however, did not change my debting habits.

My second awakening was sharp and powerful. Still oblivious to financial matters, I decided one day that I should start my own business. Not paying attention to financial details, I told my employer I would be leaving. That evening, I pored over my finances and became curious about how I might survive financially. That night I had nightmares about dinosaurs, land shifts, and impending doom. The next morning at the laundromat, I spoke to a friend about my financial concerns. He told me to stop paying my creditors, take care of myself, and start living on a cash basis. The creditors could wait.

He could have told me to walk to the edge of the earth and jump off, and I would have respected him more for his common sense. Where did this idiot live, anyway? Central Park? How could I abandon the creditors who had kept me afloat all these years, who had allowed me to vacation in Italy, who had sent me to retreats in California when I was feeling low, who fed, housed, and clothed me for fifteen years? This guy was definitely a loser and didn't know what real life required.

However, I managed to listen when he told me about Debtors Anonymous, which I attended that very afternoon. The awareness that began to dawn the night before, as I combed over some rough figures, became ever so obvious when the veil was ripped from my eyes at that first D.A. meeting. I had a problem that was well hidden beneath my monthly minimum payments. The real test was this: Could I live on a cash basis *and* pay my monthly minimums? The answer was no. This meant I would have to tell my creditors/safety net/ substitute mommy-daddy/security blankets that their usual payments would not be forthcoming as we had agreed. I heard in D.A. that my creditors would not be happy with my decision, but there were ways that I could negotiate new payment terms and eventually pay back all the creditors on my terms. "On my terms" was an interesting new concept that would take on greater meaning as I progressed through the halls of Debtors Anonymous.

I cut up all my credit cards. It was very uncomfortable, and I felt deprived and vulnerable. My credit card lines and bank loans slid into default. I was on my own to start my own business and felt terror not knowing where the next paycheck would come from. Even after having the support of D.A. for five months, I went to a credit counseling service. I had hoped to turn my bills over to the credit counseling service so they could negotiate repayment with my creditors, as another service had done before. This time, however, because of my inconsistent and unpredictable income and disproportionate debt, I could not qualify for their debt repayment plan. Instead, they gave me information on bankruptcy.

With any addiction, we truly believe we cannot leave home or live without it. The "don't leave home without it" advertisements did not prepare me for what would happen when I had charged too much. I had never left home without "it." As a matter of fact, I never left home without "them." I also had a credit line attached to my checking account, which had the same effect as hamburger helper: It added bulk without substance. This all made me feel very secure that I would be able to cope with any emergency, like taking my nephews and nieces on a boat trip before it was "too late." I never asked myself, "Too late for what?"

I heard in D.A. that debting was like an addiction. After several meetings, I came to describe addiction as a negative state; for example, if I were addicted to alcohol, drugs, or cigarettes, the absence of the substance would be felt as a deficiency. Without the substance, discomfort sets in until we regain our comfort level by using the substance. The discomfort comes from not using the addictive substance, and unwillingness to let go of it allows us to experience the tenacity of the addiction. I truly believed that neither I, nor anyone else, could live affluently without one or more credit cards or bank loans.

A warning on monthly bills might read: "If for some reason you are unable to comply with these terms and are unable to meet your monthly minimum or repay in full what you borrow, we reserve the right to turn your bill over to a collection agency that will emotionally and psychologically abuse you."

The collection agency is like a loan shark who would beat you up in the alley and threaten to murder you or your children if you don't repay the loan. The collection agency is restrained by law, but this doesn't stop them from working you over verbally on the phone, assaulting your character and attitude.

The collection agency threatened me with lawsuits and their counterpart to murder—*a bad credit rating*—without which, as we all know, we cannot live on this planet. They even said they were not lawyers and had no facts about what might happen. They just wanted to talk with me about why this happened. They talked to me as if I were a child, not letting me speak. They didn't speak about facts, only about me as a person—me as a bad person. One told me that people collecting welfare paid them more monthly than I was offering to pay. I was neither on welfare, collecting unemployment, nor employed, but it made no impression on them. They asked why I didn't have a job, what had I been doing about it. They insinuated that there was something definitely wrong with me, and they wanted to know what it was. Shame and hopelessness set in. They called a lot, never allowing much peace between their verbal batterings. The collection agency switched me from one representative to another, so no history, rapport or empathy could develop. They were just doing their job.

There is no debtor's prison, but after a few of these relentless, harassing phone calls, I wished there were. Maybe then I could escape the verbal and psychological abuse. I didn't discuss the problem with friends, because their disdain would be too demoralizing. The fear, shame, and pressure from others, and especially myself, was paralyzing.

It was a nightmarish descent into debtor's hell. I already knew I was a social misfit because I no longer had a credit card, but now I had to experience degrading humiliation because I couldn't pay my monthly minimum. So what could I do? Commit suicide? Declare bankruptcy? Leave town and change my name, leaving no forwarding phone number?

In D.A. I heard debtors contemplate suicide as their first solution to debt. When I was younger and saw old newsreels of people jumping to their death because of the 1929 stock market crash, I couldn't believe it. "Just for money?" I wondered. Now I understand it.

The next solution commonly considered is bankruptcy. For me, it was a way to relieve the harassment exerted by collection agencies. Their taunts echoed my personal guilt and the cultural disdain for such failure. Armed with the Chapter Seven escape hatch, I went to D.A. and asked other members to give me a good reason why I should not declare bankruptcy. People in D.A. told me many good reasons. Much like my previous easy way out with the consumer credit service or my first husband taking care of "loose ends," anyone who is bailed out or goes bankrupt does not learn the lessons: How to live prosperously and happily on what you earn. How to acquire peace of mind. How to live independently of credit, which we have allowed to become the master of our lives. How not to be a victim. How to negotiate your own terms and resolve your own problems.

I had only unsecured debt, and therefore nothing to sell and nothing to lose. I did not pay any creditors for six months, relying on all the tools of D.A. to prevent me from caving in and going bankrupt. The tools are the Twelve Steps and the Twelve Traditions, along with practical suggestions. I went to lots of meetings, kept penny-by-penny accounts of my spending, learned how to create spreadsheets and spending plans, and began to learn how I could feel comfortable though earning much less than I had in the past. More than anything, keeping spreadsheets on my spending and creating a monthly spending plan made me see how I had always lived in fear of lack. I saw that even if I had earned more, I would still have been fearful about not having enough. I still would have made choices that reflected my fears. D.A.'s tools taught me how to make choices and feel more in control.

The biggest lesson I learned was that by relying on a Power greater than myself, I could let go of the fear. It was the fear that hurt me the most. I was often sick during that first year of D.A.; my stomach was in knots most of the time. For ten months in a row, on the first of the month, I had zero dollars in my checking account. But for ten months in a row, I was able to pay my rent, phone and electric bills, buy groceries, see a movie, and visit friends. The difference between my first month and the tenth month is that in the beginning I had been riddled with fear, could not sleep, was obsessed about money, and could not see a way out. After ten months, one day I looked at my zero-balance checkbook, shrugged my shoulders and had a nice day. That night at a meeting I realized my fear had lifted. Money no longer could control how I felt or dictate to me if I was going to appreciate the positive things in my life. Removing fear of financial insecurity from my life is the greatest gift to me from D.A.

Eventually, with help from my D.A. friends, I began paying my creditors, sometimes only $10 or $15 a month . . . whatever was left after I took care of myself. Eventually, my creditors realized I would probably pay them back, and the harassing phone calls and threats subsided. As my business grew and my income became more steady and reliable, I increased my monthly payments to creditors.

It's been five years now since I entered D.A. and stopped using credit cards. Today I owe $8,000 compared to the original $25,259 of debt. My father forgave his loan to me. I negotiated a two-year payment plan to pay back my overdue taxes. I consolidated and refinanced my personal bank loans for a better interest rate and more manageable monthly payments. All of my retail store debts are paid off. My business is booming, and my current plan is to retire all of my debt in sixteen months. I didn't have to hide behind an agency that would talk to my creditors for me. No matter how fearful I was of the collection agencies, I learned that they couldn't really hurt me. Even if they had sued me, which none did, a court hearing wouldn't have frightened me. I am now certain that not only can I repay all of my debt, but I will be able to save money instead of paying enormous amounts of interest. It's a miracle.

Since coming to D.A., I have paid my rent and utilities every month, eaten well, enjoyed vacations and entertainment, returned to graduate school to finish my master's degree, and paid cash for everything including my computer and spreadsheet software. The spreadsheet allows me to keep a penny by penny account of my finances and reveals a great deal about the choices I make in my life. I also learned that a debit card, which looks and acts like a credit card but deducts the purchase amount directly from my personal checking account, takes care of car rentals, hotel reservations, and other purchases that require plastic.

The big difference is not in the lesser dollar amount I owe, but rather that since D.A., I have lived on a cash basis, after fifteen years of the illusion that credit cards were taking care of me. In fact, I had been taking care of the lending institutions by paying so much interest. The focus of D.A. is taking care of myself. D.A. taught me that if I didn't learn to take care of myself, then I could not take care of anyone else. Without D.A. I would not have been able to reverse the process of incurring debt or learn how to live a debt-free and prosperous life. My peace of mind became essential to the process, and I needed my supportive and understanding program friends. They too have felt the embarrassment and humiliation of being in the same place . . . in debt.

I as a debtor was not guilty, per se. I did, however, have to take responsibility for changing my self-destructive behavior. I needed help in a nonjudgmental, safe place. I have the benefit of D.A., for without it I never would have been able to let go of my credit cards overnight. Without D.A., I never would have trusted myself to survive without a line of credit. In D.A. I learned to manage my money, no matter how much or how little. Although I started out hoping I would be one of those in the Fellowship who triples income or becomes rich, I realize that at whatever level I earn money, I can make choices about whether or not I will enjoy abundance in my life. No longer is there a false sense of security based on any person, place, circumstance, or line of credit. The saying "The best things in life are free" is no longer an empty cliché.

To believe that I could live without debting took a leap of faith from the common beliefs in this society, beliefs that are bolstered by a lot of advertising about things I should want or need and about the credit lines that will get them.

My freedom becomes greater every day, because I make choices about what I really need to live fully and what is important: my well-being, joy, and peace.

Originally published in the first edition of *A Currency of Hope.*

22

~~~~~

The Escape Artist

This debtor created only prisons until he learned to use the D.A. Tools.

My problems with money literally began in my childhood, but I will fast-forward to the summer after my thirty-third birthday. My girl-friend, whom I had become financially indebted to and dependent on, kicked me out. After the breakup of the relationship, a generous and compassionate friend took me into her one-room apartment. There I slept on the floor on a convertible mattress and tried to pull my life together during the day, while she was at work. I was a member of Al-Anon and A.A. and went to Twelve-Step meetings day and night, just to keep from going out of my mind. You see, in addition to feeling devastated by the end of the relationship, I had no income except a modest unemployment check every two weeks. I had no money to move, to pay for rent, to pay for anything beyond groceries and transportation. I knew of D.A., but I was trying to hold on for dear life. Who had time for another Twelve-Step program?

The only good news, or so I thought, was that I had moved, and none of my creditors knew where I was. You see, over the years I managed to ac-cumulate more than thirty creditors to whom I owed more than $13,000. I was always temporarily relieved when I moved, which was frequently, and could escape the mail for a while. I got into debt by doing things like run-ning up a long-distance phone bill for more than $1,000, not paying it, and then switching companies. I would also take out loans, embellishing the applications, to meet living expenses and spend the money rapidly without any means of paying them back. In addition, I hadn't paid taxes for five years, hadn't filed for an additional five years, and owed the government another $30,000 or so, and I got notices every month. I was definitely on the run. For the moment though, my friend's floor was the only place I had to go. The only solace I had was that very few people knew where I was. When they found me, I would ignore them.

It was hard to believe I was hiding again. I was used to it. My other Twelve-Step experiences had yet to correct this character defect. Regarding money and responsibility, the mailbox had long been my enemy. Everyone wanted something I couldn't give. It got so I could not bear to go near the mailbox without intense fear. I actually accumulated over 175 pieces of unopened mail. I thought if I didn't open it, I was safe from problems I couldn't bear to face.

A week or two after moving in with my friend, I did begin, with great resistance, to look for work. I did so for more than two months, but the results were dismal and depressing. Maybe my attitude had something to do with it. My friend was clearly and understandably feeling the stress of having two persons in such a small space. I was in despair. I knew I could not stay with my friend indefinitely, but I couldn't afford to move. My job search was at a dead end. I needed money and time was ticking away. I have always been an escape artist, escaping every problem I've ever gotten into, but this one wasn't so easy.

Somehow I came up with the idea to make money for another getaway by holding a conference and charging people to attend. If successful, it would give me enough money to depart and find a little financial breathing space. Now in order to pull it off, I had to use my friend's phone constantly and turned her apartment into my office. In talking my friend into this arrangement, I was very convincing, like most escape artists. At this point, she grudgingly agreed, believing it would help me move out. Just about a week after I began working on this conference that would "save" me, the tension between us began to mount. I was doing my best to keep the activity in her apartment to a minimum, but the wheels were in motion for the conference. This continued for three months of constant phone calls, planning, papers everywhere. That I was overstaying my welcome is the understatement of the century. A combination of hard work and good luck made the conference a modest financial success. Looking back, I know my Higher Power was taking care of me.

As you might guess, the moment the conference was over, my friend, by now sitting on built-up frustration, asked when I was moving. In a sense, she became another creditor, wanting to know when was I going to take care of the problem. There was nowhere to run now; I was living with a "creditor." I felt a lot of pain and resentment toward her. I had not one second to enjoy my triumph, not one day to relax after the ordeal of the conference. My anger felt justified. My distorted thoughts told me that when I was down, people owed me a break, their understanding and compassion, though I gave little in return. How dare she take this attitude with me! In retrospect, I see how self-centered, arrogant, and fearful I was. Now I had been asked by another woman to leave, just like my girlfriend before her.

This was a terrible reminder of how lost I was. Though I had a little money, I didn't know where I could go, because it wouldn't last. With no stable income and just a few strained friendships, it's no wonder why. I had no real prospects, my creditor and IRS problems were overwhelming, and I didn't know where to turn. The cumulative pain of all the years of running fell heavily upon me, and I could no longer escape. I felt tortured, and leaving this world crossed my mind.

Two days after my friend asked me to move, I somehow remembered D.A. A Twelve-Step comrade had told me about D.A. many months earlier, and I had gone to one meeting then, but I thought "those people" were all nuts. Asking me to write down everything I spent! Sitting down with others and having them suggest how I should spend my money! Keeping records of whom I owe money to! I left that meeting saying that they were all "anal retentive." This time I went to meetings willing to listen. My intense pain had finally made me ready for something, anything. Desperation made me more reasonable. I now thank my Higher Power for this pain, because when I get crazy, and it still happens, pain makes me willing. Willingness has become the key to my recovery.

When I became willing to write down my numbers, translated to looking at the truth, I began to spend less. When I became willing to do spreadsheets, translated to identifying my true needs, I saw that I was not a compulsive spender. I discovered that I was not spending recklessly as I had believed, but had been underearning and couldn't meet my reasonable expenses. In fact, I was underspending in essential areas like the dentist, doctor, clothes, vacation, etc.

Those things had been for others, not me. When I became willing to become solvent and stay that way no matter how scary, other options that I could have never dreamed of came to me. More than anything, when I became willing to go to meetings, make phone calls, and listen to the suggestions from a Pressure Relief Group, my entire outlook changed.

Through the suggestions of a Pressure Relief Group, I began consulting with someone, charging them for my expertise. Though I had skills and talents to offer, I had been using them to scheme and get around life. Yet, this time I was using my assets with integrity. So my one client and I were going along fine, and I was doing office work and a few other things to make money. How convenient is my memory. I was also illegally on unemployment. I thought it was OK to collect unemployment and work "off the books" because I needed to survive. It kept me underearning and living on the edge, not helping my confidence one bit. But thankfully, I eventually got out of this trap. Here's how.

I was scrimping to get by, also working the program, but I wasn't willing to let go of my unemployment game. In a Pressure Relief Group I was asked if I was setting money aside for taxes from my consultant income. I was shocked. "I can't," I answered. I vaguely knew I should be setting aside a tax fund, but how could I when only making $50 some weeks? How could I take $15 of that and put it aside?

Under their gentle but persistent guidance, I agreed to take out 30% of every consulting check and set it aside for taxes, *no matter what*. I was afraid to do this with every bone in my body. I had hidden from the IRS for years, and there was no money to pay *Them*, the IRS, the bad guys. Now money I needed to live on was going to them. But as we discussed in the Pressure Relief Group, taking the money out was not only to stay out of tax debt, it was also to demonstrate my willingness for a Higher Power to replace it and somehow meet my needs. This was my first test of acting on faith, trusting the wisdom of others. After that, with each and every check, I kept 30% for taxes.

With this act of willingness, and others like it, my life changed drastically. I received more abundance than I believed possible. I am not even sure why. It's the demonstration of faith that made a difference. When I survived and more money began to come in through my actions, it seemed miraculous. Why, oh why, had I resisted for so long? Oh sure, I had fantasies of financial stability, but never really believed I could achieve financial comfort, pay off my debts, or stop living on the "edge." Maybe my Higher Power needed for me to learn something first, and then by example, teach others. When I became willing to hold 30% and listen to the common wisdom of D.A., my life got better and better, and it still does.

Since coming into D.A., I have opened those stockpiled envelopes. Now I open my mail every day. I no longer fear, but actually look forward to my mail. By the way, inside two unopened envelopes were checks made out to me. Now I have filed all back taxes, and I am making an offer to the IRS to eradicate my debt. I pay quarterly taxes. I have paid ten creditors and make payments to others regularly. I know they will all eventually be paid. I have increased my income more than 75% over the last two years, and I save money every week. When I visited my family in the Midwest, I paid for my plane ticket and had the money to stay at a hotel, rent a car and even to treat my nieces and nephew.

Writing this brings tears to my eyes, because every year on every visit, I stayed at my parents' home, borrowed their cars, and was ashamed about how little I had to spend. Now I could go home as an adult. My mother said to me, "How much is the plane ticket?" and I said, "Don't worry. I'm paying for it." She said, "Well, you know I can't come to see you in New York, so that's why your Dad and I send you money." "I know," I said, "but I'll take care of it. I'm fine. You spend it on yourself." She started to cry. Finally, money was not an obstacle between us. There was room now for feelings and growth. I can't overstate the power of this moment in my life.

My parents had come from Depression-era households. They never gave themselves much of anything and long suffered from financial and emotional deprivation. When, as a boy, I asked for 25 cents a week allowance, they said they couldn't afford it. Even then, I knew they could, but they were telling me there wasn't enough. My insanity with money and debt is evident in my belief that there isn't, and never will be, enough. My parents never felt they had enough. They couldn't give me what they couldn't give themselves—even 25 cents given with love and abundance was threatening. Willingness to come to D.A. and show up has released me from the corrosive and despairing attitudes my family and countless other families experienced.

From a poor, struggling household, from the floor of a one-room apartment, I have gone on to a great place to live, stable income, a thriving new business, and I move toward my vision proactively. I no longer wait for my money to run out before I take action. I have overcome, one day at a time, my almost terminal procrastination. My actions and money flow more freely. My creditors and Uncle Sam know where I live. I have six separate savings funds set aside for vacations, luxuries, investments, taxes, professional expenses, and a personal prudent reserve. I show up despite the fears that occasionally still run through me when I think it may all come to an end. The difference is that before D.A., things did run out: money, opportunity, friends, and love. Since D.A., abundance never runs out. In short, I have learned to begin taking care of myself. My other Twelve-Step experiences are more rich when I keep the focus on myself. As I take care of what I can and leave the rest to my Higher Power, I have everything I need, and more. For the first time in my life, with D.A.'s help, today is much brighter and freer, and I look ahead to a promising future.

Even though I have been in other programs, I have never *felt* the existence of a loving Higher Power before. Now I do. Even when I struggle, I know I am being looked after. I know when I am willing, God makes all things possible. I still get angry, play out old habits, and I still have character defects, like intolerance, blaming, controlling, or acting out of fear. Very recently I have taken time to pray for the people I resent or to affirm what I am grateful for so I don't hang onto the feeling. It's human to get angry, scared, judgmental, but I don't live in it. I learned much of this from reading the A.A. "Big Book," something else I became willing to do.

I am truly grateful for what I have received since coming to D.A. I still have bouts with distressing feelings and self-centered fear, but I have others to help me get out of myself and into life. I have abundance, friends, greater feelings of self-worth and self-love—greater sense of purpose. I have more than enough money for today, and I have myself. Without D.A. I do not know where I would be, but now I know where I can go. Believe me, I was and still am afraid to try things that have been suggested. It's tough to leave all the familiar deprivation behind. With D.A., that is healing. Now I know that if I demonstrate my willingness, even the smallest amount, my Higher Power will lead me to abundance and grace. Whatever God is, God speaks through D.A. I am grateful I became willing to listen.

Originally published in the first edition of *A Currency of Hope.*

23

From Homelessness to Happiness

*She finds a new D.A. community to support her
in her recovery from compulsive debting.*

July 7, 2008, was my twenty-year anniversary in Debtors Anonymous. If I were looking at my life from the vantage point of myself twenty years ago, I would be amazed. I have a husband I love, we are building a house in Vermont, and I have been successfully and professionally self-employed for seven years.

Twenty years ago I lived in Boston. I was sleeping on the floor of my ex-boyfriend's apartment with no job, no home, and no money of my own. I was twenty-nine years old and harbored a great sense of inferiority, particularly in relation to my older sister, who had all of those things. I grew up in a family in which people were expected to excel. In fact, I had done well in college and went immediately on to graduate school. At the continual prodding of my father, I finished a Ph.D. in psychology. All the while I had no sense of self-esteem. I drank, used drugs, and barely got through. I was always terrified that I would not be able to complete my work, which required maturity and sanity.

I don't know how I had gotten to be the debtor I was at twenty-nine. I was a happy child up until third grade. My parents often fought about money and parenting. I didn't get along with my mother, but I was very close to my father. Then one day my father came home from work and found me fighting with my mother. He went into a rage at me, packed all my clothes in a suitcase, which he put outside, and told me to leave. I'm sure he never really meant for me to leave the family, but I didn't know that, and I had some type of a nervous breakdown, which led to getting sick for three months with a temperature that kept going up and down. This led to chronic depression. And I now felt that I was an outcast. I don't think my parents caught on to how unhappy I had become. I learned quickly how to fake it after that. I didn't believe in myself and my abilities. I was jealous of others and felt inferior.

After graduate school in California I moved to Boston with my boyfriend. He was unemployed; I was working at two low-paying jobs. We couldn't make ends meet. I had never used a credit card, but had one during school that my father had given me for emergencies. My boyfriend talked me into using it. I quickly began spending money that was not my own. My father gave us some money in addition.

When I broke up with this man I became very isolated. I could not make friends. I always felt desperate and inferior on the inside, even though I worked hard to have people see me as competent on the outside. I had a spiritual awakening of the worst kind in 1986 at twenty-nine years old when I crashed up my brand new Toyota Corolla SR5. No one was hurt, but I finally realized that life was not working for me. I was miserable and hopeless. I quit my job and began to take money from my father (to my mother's dismay). I could not support myself and eventually lost my apartment.

I went to a career counselor and by some strange set of circumstances met a woman in a Twelve-Step program. She took me to my first (non-D.A.) Twelve-Step meeting. The day my ex-boyfriend asked me to leave his house (after three months of sleeping on his floor) I was at a Twelve-Step meeting, when a man began talking to me about Debtors Anonymous. I knew right away that was what I needed, and took down the meeting information.

D.A. miracles started happening for me right away when I agreed to stop debting one day at a time and stop taking money from my father. I got a temp job right away. It was at a hospital in Cambridge, Massachusetts, where seriously brain-injured people had permanent housing. (I could easily identify with their mental condition!) There I ate meals for $1 and drank coffee for 25 cents. I was there for six months and got paid $9 an hour, which was enough to pay my meager bills. I had lucked into a funky apartment overlooking the ocean for only $200 a month, and was able to support myself for the first time in two years.

My first Pressure Relief Group wanted me now to get a permanent secretarial job. It was easy to be a temp secretary, but to be a REAL secretary was a major blow to my ego. After all, I had a Ph.D. in psychology! That was one of my first surrenders in D.A. There would be many more over the years. God's will, not my will, was not something that has ever come easily to me.

Over the next three and a half years I attended D.A. meetings regularly and grew tremendously as a person. I was working at Massachusetts General Hospital and got into my first relationship in recovery. But slowly I started getting irritated by other people's character defects, stopped going to meetings, and eventually moved away from D.A. The only good thing I did that indeed kept me solvent for the next five years was to use a Spending Plan. I am a huge believer in them because this was the key to remaining solvent in spite of starting to make bad choices for myself. I let my father buy me a car and give me money for some living expenses during the next several years. He decided to take out a loan at almost $500 a month, which was in my name and which I could never afford on my own. (But I did take it over after returning to D.A., and it took an excruciating amount of time to sell the damn car!)

I moved to Vermont with a fiancé in 1996. The engagement did not work out, but I ended up remaining in Vermont and meeting a woman who wanted to start D.A. in Montpelier. We had regular meetings for the next six months. The next year I moved to Burlington and joined with a group of people who were also trying hard to get D.A. off the ground. I was back in the center of the program! It has been about eight years since I have once again been attending D.A. regularly, doing service and working a program. I have been a slow grower in the program. But I finally got one of my visions—to be married—at forty-nine years old! I still remain solvent and am making more money in my chosen profession, psychology, than I ever have before. I carry a high level of responsibility, something prior to D.A. I felt incapable of. I live with much less anxiety about money, although it does come and go. I am just beginning to develop a retirement plan, something others in D.A. were better at doing earlier in their lives and programs. I have many friends in and out of the program and consider my D.A. community to be my family. I have known many of them for five to eight years now, and enjoy watching each one of them recover and add new successes to their lives.

We have an active group in Burlington. We have a Do-D.A. Day event every fall and a Winter Lights recovery celebration in the winter. We have high attendance at D.A. retreats in August and April. But mostly we support each other in staying solvent one day at a time and living lives that are filled with joy and satisfaction. Thank God for D.A.!

Originally published in the 2008 second-quarter issue of *Ways & Means* as "Twenty Years of D.A. Recovery—What a Ride!" Revised and posted on the Debtors Anonymous website as "From Homelessness to Happiness: A D.A. Odyssey."

24

From Fruitless to Fulfilled
in D.A. and B.D.A.

"Who was I to say that God would not restore me to
sanity around my business and my income?"

What it was like . . . what happened . . . what it is like today:
I felt like I was dying on the vine, again. I slogged home in April
2002 after another day of fruitless toil, full of despair. That evening, I prayed
to God, or maybe whined is a more apt term: "God, I can't believe that you
brought me from destitution, prostitution, and hopelessness to this misery."

Eight months before, I had left a successful career of twenty-eight years to
try something different, and it was not working. I am a fortunate person when
it comes to jobs; every job interview I had ever gone on had resulted in a job
offer. This time, I sent out eighty-four resumes and did not get so much as a
call back, much less an interview. I felt completely desolate.

Several events then transpired, leaving me with the sense that I was supposed to start my own consulting business. I have never been a person with
any desire to start my own business; my mother died homeless and I have
always had safe, secure, well-paying jobs. I worked my way through college
(took me eleven years) and then four years of law school at night, working full
time, and certainly was a self-starter, but I was not interested in beginning a

business. My sense from God was, "Fine, looks like you have limited my options—you won't go where I am leading you, but you don't want to stay where you are." I felt helpless. Finally, after journaling, writing up a business plan, and working with my D.A. sponsor, I was ready to step off the cliff and leave the six-figure salary to start my own business.

As background, on November 8, 1990, I went to my first meeting of Debtors Anonymous, and while it was a relatively "high bottom," I owed $47,000 and change in unsecured debt. I wanted what you had, and kept coming back and following suggestions. On April 17, 1991, I had my first Pressure Relief Group (back then in Virginia we called them "P Groups"). From then I put one foot in front of the other, did the steps in a slow and deliberate manner with a wonderful sponsor, and continued to have PRGs every three months. When my career moved me across the country, I kept working with both my sponsor and the PRG, as miracles continued to happen. I paid off all outstanding debt, and began living a prosperous life with an abundant spending plan. That is my D.A. story in a nutshell. I had not given Business Debtors Anonymous a thought. That all was to change, dramatically.

I had saved up eight months of expenses before leaving the job of fruitless toil; it helped every day to know when I would be leaving, and why I was doing that job. I prepared a business plan, started having monthly PRGs, researched office equipment, got a business license, opened a business checking account, had a fabulous logo and web page designed by my generous sister, ordered business cards, and prayed . . . did I mention prayer? I worked with my PRG to significantly reduce my spending plan (we called it a temporary spending plan—alas, no more $440 a month for a vacation fund!).

(Now I recommend to everyone who asks for my experience, strength, and hope on this issue to have one year of expenses in savings, as things got pretty dicey at eight months.) When I left the job, I was full of gratitude and fear.

What did I do? I worked the Steps of D.A. I was powerless over my fear of economic insecurity and my life was unmanageable. Every day, fear grabbed me, and every day I prayed and wrestled away from it. From my experience, I knew that God would restore me to sanity around having my own business. I turned my will and my life over to the care of God as I understood God. I prepared a daily schedule template with a set time each day for marketing (two hours), business strategy development (one hour), actual work (three hours—in the beginning I didn't actually have any work for this time, so I volunteered), and appreciation (one hour for handwritten thank you notes to everyone who spoke with me).

I filled my office with inspiring statements or pictures ("What will I carry today, will it be fear or faith?"; "Wonder Woman Works Here"; mission/vision statements such as "I bring spirituality, integrity, and competence into joyful service of others"; "I earn bountiful income from vibrant, appreciative people who are pleased to pay.") Every day I meditated to put myself in a loving, grateful place. To manage the fear, I said, "OK, fear, you have ten minutes today; go crazy" and I would awfulize for the ten minutes and then say, "Thank you for sharing. Now I have to get to work."

If fear came up during the day, I would say, "Oh, you had your chance earlier, and you will again tomorrow. Right now I have to think about something else," and I would pray. Every day I would look and see the fear or faith question and I would say, "OK, today I am going to pretend that I am a woman of faith. What would a woman of faith do at this moment?" and I would get into action.

B.D.A. meetings helped immensely, reminding me of the powerful tools of the program and business debting issues. Hearing others share their experience, strength, and hope has been invaluable to me. If nothing else, I get to laugh out loud at myself. (And frequently! "Those who laugh at themselves will never cease to be amused.")

Service is also an important part of my program, which I believe is essential to my recovery. B.D.A. and my experience with D.A. demonstrated the importance of accurate and up-to-date record keeping, and I have been rigorous with my numbers.

I don't think I completely internalized the Second and Third Steps until I began my business. I wrote a long time on the Second Step, and all the insanity God had restored me from in so many areas of my life. After all this evidence, who was I to say that God would not restore me to sanity around my business and my income?

Since 1986, I had been turning my will and my life over to the care of God in a variety of areas. But I had never left my career up to God, since that was an area that, at least from outward appearances, was a success. I was truly on my knees and went on blind faith, doing the footwork and leaving the results to God. I was almost in a panic toward the end of the eight months, and was willing to sell my house when the evidence of miracles began to manifest.

That was four years ago. The results came. Although my business currently does not resemble my initial business plan, my income is greater than it ever was. My spending plan is no longer austere, but is abundant again. While I have not yet achieved a prudent reserve that is six months of my "nut" (monthly personal and business expenses), I am working steadily toward that, often two steps forward and one back, and am confident that I will reach that point.

My business has expanded in unforeseen ways, such that I have had two business/vacation trips to Europe and one to Asia in the last year, with more planned. I take eight weeks of vacation every year to wonderful places, sometimes for touring, sometimes for relaxation. I go on a retreat and have a "spa day" once per quarter, a result of a PRG assignment to write a plan for preserving my business' prime asset, which is me. I am funding a personal retirement plan and take great joy in paying myself first. I have a rich life with countless blessings, many people who love me, a home I love (even when major repairs are needed, such as an air conditioning system and dry-rot repair), fascinating work that compensates me well, and a relationship with God that nourishes me daily.

I am truly blessed. Thank you, D.A. and B.D.A.!

Originally posted on the Debtors Anonymous website as "A D.A./B.D.A. Journey: From Fruitless to Fulfilled."

25

Twenty-one Years of Solvency

Working the Steps and staying solvent bring her
out of darkness to discover her real self.

I stumbled into a D.A. meeting in New York City with the idea of one or two meetings before I left the city to share life in Boston with my latest love. I'd been telling a friend what I was up to: "Well, heck, he should buy me a car" and "He'll have to take care of me and provide for me, as I'm the one moving." This wise angel suggested I consider not starting a new relationship on lies, and to go to Debtors Anonymous for a couple of meetings before leaving. "Me! In Debtors Anonymous? No way! I don't have money issues." She gently nudged again, "You'll get clarity on things. A couple of meetings will help square it away for you." I went.

Little did I know it would not be for a couple of meetings, it would be for twenty-one years worth of meetings, embracing a solvent life; that not only would I get clarity, but that I would not go to Boston. Thus began my love affair with D.A., and the beginning of the agony and the ecstasy.

I was born into the belly of the "not enough" syndrome. Not only did my family not have enough, my community didn't have enough, and my nation of origin, England, did not have enough. I was born during World War II, in a bomb shelter during an air raid, and with victory by the Allies came out-and-out poverty for the English working class. Not having enough was a usual experience.

With it, however, for me, came the skills of manipulation, coercion, thievery, deception, and hoarding. I used them well. I could look you in the eyes with money stashed away here and there, and convince you I had not one single penny. I held on tight to my hoard because I truly believed there wasn't enough out there, and that if I let go, it would all vanish. And, of course, what I believed was what I created, and thus I lived out my reality. A good source of easy resources were men, and I fished for wealthy men. It didn't matter if they were married; it only mattered what car they drove, did they have money, and would they spend it on me? I was empty, cardboard-like, with no depth, a malcontent living a futile way of life in fear and despair, which inevitably led to addictions to cover the pain, and endless broken relationships to supply me with my fix—money. I bottomed out homeless and later ended up living in the Salvation Army.

I had not one idea of what psychology was running my life, though I was an educated woman with a degree. One man told me to be myself. What the heck was he talking about? I was living in the depth of darkness in New York City, scrounging at the Salvation Army and plotting to embark on yet another addictive provider relationship when I came into the D.A. rooms.

Something began to stir in my soul. At that time I could not tell you why I delayed the departure to Boston, but I did. Now I know Holy Spirit was rising. My time had come to answer the call, or not. The fear escalated in the beginning when I began making the discoveries. Oh, the shame I felt, the disgust at myself, the appalling, stunning refusal to accept what I was beginning to get clear about. I wept, felt more lost than ever; I went into nightmare depressions, and then—another miracle. The only place I felt safe was in those D.A. rooms.

The terror gradually faded only by keeping close to D.A., and so I began to find my True Self. I began to know that the Source of my abundance was within, that the degree to which I understood my Source of All manifests my material world and emotional experience of my life on this Earth. The Twelve Steps nurtured an aliveness of my living experience, and were the vehicle for a viable and very real contact with the Holy Spirit for me. The D.A. Tools became such practical actions that seemingly answered in some way, shape, or form every problem I confronted. I began to grow my own resources, and I began to accrue my own generated material wealth.

From homelessness to multiple property ownership, visions were coming true because I believed they could. And what you believe is what you get, right? (Aha—but only the Fourth Step really uncovered what I truly, darkly believed deep down.) There can be no slack on my part. There can only be applied vigilance and ever-awakening, because the fear, the dark force, could seep back in. If I slacken I stand a chance of becoming lost again, and I am consciously choosing not to.

I have a sponsor in my life to help me; my well-wisher, my mentor, my grounding. Oh what joy to have such an individual instantly there, loving, caring, and suggesting. Now, living the Twelve-Step way of life has released a life's purpose for me of helping others, of carrying the message of hope to those despairing, that same hope that was given to me those long twenty-one years ago. This is my life. D.A. is my life.

Originally published in the 2008 second-quarter issue of *Ways & Means* as "She Came for a Night and Stayed Twenty-one Years."

26

⁓

The Good Old Days:
A Fond Look Back

D.A. was his last resort. It became his first investment.

One Sunday about seven years ago, I awoke from a long, dreamless sleep and found myself $20,117.96 in debt—to six credit cards, many friends, student loans, my bank, and to my nemesis, the Department of Motor Vehicles.

I didn't know how it all had happened. I was truly mystified. All I knew was that I was a trustworthy and decent human being, that I had not intentionally set out to make friends and total strangers upset, impatient, frustrated, and angry with me. I never seriously entertained the idea of running out on my debts or "beating" my creditors; I had every intention of repaying money I borrowed and spent. I believed that a combination of unfortunate circumstances—a bad childhood, a few bad relationships, an illness, car problems, a job loss, graduate school, a career change, a lousy job market, and an eventual low-paying job—had made it impossible for me to avoid going into debt. In sum, I was the most misunderstood and maligned person on earth.

On the other hand, I knew exactly how it had all happened. By the time I was out of college, I was already bouncing checks and borrowing against credit cards. I had never lived where I paid the rent on time. My mood-changing shopping sprees, my spending for status, my poor financial judgment, my equating love with money, my anxious wait for the Big Fix, my denial, my rationalizations—all these and more I knew to be true on a gut level, but they hadn't reached my soul yet.

I didn't know what to do. Terrified, I was literally penniless. I had incoming bills that I couldn't pay, a car that was out of gas and needed maintenance, and an empty refrigerator. Believe me, I tried to borrow more money. Though on some level I knew it was impossible to get out of debt by borrowing more money, all that concerned me then was basic survival. Borrowing was the only way I knew to get by. I begged my bank to lend me more money; I pleaded with my credit card companies to raise my credit limits (how humiliating!), but my efforts were in vain. No one would lend me another dime. My "debt-to-income ratio" was too high. And now as I look back, that was a blessing in disguise.

I had known of Debtors Anonymous for nearly a year before I joined. I first heard of it in a graduate course on addictions and substance abuse. "Hmmm, Debtors Anonymous," I mused somewhat sarcastically. "Sounds like something I could use." Purely out of curiosity I decided to attend a meeting, but as fate would have it, when I arrived I learned the meeting had been moved to another location. Deciding a late arrival would be too embarrassing, I opted to return the next week. As it happened, I returned the next year. Again, as I look back, I was not meant to go to that first meeting. I was still in the heyday of my debting and hadn't hit bottom yet. "D.A. is my last resort," I told myself. "If I really screw up, then I'll go." And did I screw up!

That following year, I attended my first D.A. meeting. I was extremely arrogant. In retrospect, I don't know how anyone put up with me. I thought that my expenses were extraordinary, that I wasn't some deadbeat who didn't pay my bills: Once I graduated and got a real job I'd really rake in the bucks. Hell, I'd show them! I didn't keep a spending record or have a spending plan, and I still used credit cards. Even outside of D.A., all I ever talked about were bills and money.

Gradually, however, things began to change. I was starting to internalize what I heard at meetings. This was not conscious—I was listening with my soul. Outside of D.A., in my other life, I noticed subtle differences in my thinking. I wasn't so uptight and impatient, so bitter and resentful. Amazed, I eventually realized that I wasn't doing anything that I enjoyed. No wonder

I was so depressed and lethargic! Either I was doing what I thought others expected of me, or I was living for others because of my inability to set boundaries, or I was debting to take my feelings away.

D.A. taught me these truths: Just because I don't have everything I want doesn't mean I have nothing, money can't buy what money can't buy, and it just couldn't buy what I was missing. Spending to fill that soul emptiness wasn't going to work. Instead, I filled my soul emptiness with actions and quickly discovered that the emptiness closed up. Now I enjoy what is mine, both my material possessions and my personal attributes. My life has become fulfilled.

My debts, the reason I came to D.A., are slowly coming under control. I have negotiated repayment agreements with my personal creditors, took forbearances on my student loans, and paid off every outstanding parking violation. I have a commitment not to incur any new debts. My personal bank loan was paid up last week. I glowed as I wrote the last check. I paid off five of my six credit cards; four of them had reached the limits. Now the cards are destroyed, and my accounts are closed. Instead of the fear and defeat I anticipated when I cut up the cards, I felt freedom and relief. I have liquidated over $4,000 of my debts at this point, all without any sense of deprivation. I even went on a much-needed two-week vacation and paid in cash. I keep a daily spending record and a monthly spending plan, tools I scoffed at when I first came to D.A. Strangely, I never realized how much I actually earned until recently.

All of these gifts are beyond my wildest dreams. When I was debting, my life consisted entirely of deprivation and pressure, but this trip down memory lane has been revealing and rewarding. Now I know how far I've come in ten months of D.A. recovery and how far I still have to go. This journey has not been easy. All of my character defects and compulsions revolve around money. Through D.A., I learned that money itself is not the problem. The real problem is the issues money brings up. Transforming my miserable existence into a meaningful life is nothing short of miraculous. Now I can look forward to the future instead of dreading it. I'll live better, not worse, than I did in the old days. And for these gifts I have D.A. to thank.

Originally published in the first edition of *A Currency of Hope*.

27

A Onetime Liar and Cheat
Finds a New Life

From living off others to a fulfilling, prosperous life of honor and dignity.

My story is not unlike a lot of others before me. I was raised in an affluent suburb of a major U.S. city. I had one sibling—an older sister—and we were spoiled rotten.

My father made an excellent income and we had all we wanted, when we wanted it. My father's story is an interesting one and is part of mine. He was a Depression kid. He had to work—and work hard—for all he wanted. He was determined that his family would never have to do that. Here is one example of some of the unusual things my father would do: he would use a napkin five times so as not to waste it, but in the same breath spend $60,000 on a boat for him and my mom to cruise around on.

My mother also worked and had "her" money separate from the "family's" money. My model on how to deal with money was screwed up when I saw these things happening.

Needless to say, I had no formal training from either of my parents on how to deal with money. My dad would joke with me and say if I wanted more money, to get another job, but in all reality he wasn't kidding. I had a paper route when I was ten years old just to keep my dad quiet. But whenever I needed money, my mom would give me some. I learned at an early age how to manipulate my parents to get money out of them. All I needed to do was to get some tears flowing and BANG—money!

That was my M.O. I worked part-time through high school, just as all teenagers did. Of course, there was never enough money so I would always go to mom and ask for some cash and she would say every time, "You know you really should learn to handle your money better, but here you go." BANG—money!

I also did some pretty rotten things. I would steal money from my mom's purse, my dad's wallet, and from the money stashes I found that my parents kept around the house. I also stole from department stores and other shops. The big question is why? I got all the clothes and other things I ever wanted from my parents. Why did I need to steal? It was a great question, one that I didn't get the answer to until I later worked the Steps of D.A. It was to fill a hole, a hole that was there because my dad was never around, always working; a hole that was there because I was a loner and didn't have a lot of friends. Because of D.A. I now know why those holes were there, and today I fill them with program.

As I got older the stealing stopped and I went away to college. My college was paid for in full by my parents. Although today I appreciate the fact that they paid for it all, it's just another example of how I felt I was deserving of everything. While away at a state college I made the decision to come home. I'm not sure why—I just did not feel that the school was for me. I transferred to a school near my home. While I was living back at home I moved into an apartment in a building that my father owned. I was the "maintenance man" of the building—I mowed the lawn, shoveled the sidewalks and changed fuses when needed. The best part was I was living rent-free!

After graduating from college and getting a job, I had no idea what to do with the money I was earning. I had no knowledge of how to save, budget, etc. I just spent it as soon as I got it. I'd grown up that way, so why not continue? My mom continued to buy my groceries, and pay my electric and phone bills. It was the old story—spoiled rotten kid grows into spoiled rotten adult.

One day a credit card application arrived in the mail. Since it seemed that I needed a credit card, I filled out the application and sent it in. Two weeks later I got my card and was off to the races. I found a grocery store that would take a credit card for groceries, so I charged my groceries. I kept charging things until I got to my limit and could charge no more. I would pay the minimums, but that was all.

When I had had enough I would invite myself to my parents' house for dinner (you see what's coming, don't you?), enjoy a nice dinner, and as dessert was served and my dad asked the question all parents ask, "How are things?" my tears would well up and I would explain that I couldn't pay my credit card bill and that I had cut up the card and would never use one again. BANG—a check would be written for the balance! Once I had check in hand I was out of there. This went on for years, although I eventually did stop. I'm not sure why. Perhaps HP intervened and temporarily restored me to sanity.

So let's recap the story so far:

- Spoiled Rotten Kid—Spoiled Rotten Adult

- Got Anything I Wanted

- Lived on My Own—Got into Debt

- Parents Bailed Me Out

   Now, there's a healthy lifestyle!

In 1981 I met a wonderful woman, and we were married in 1983. When we got married I was debt-free. In 1985 we started our family with the birth of our first daughter, and in 1987 our second daughter. This is where my spending and debting started up again. I wanted to give my daughters everything they wanted because that is the way I thought it worked. I started hiding money from my wife, lying on expense reports, lying to my wife on how I got the extra money, etc.

In 1991 our third daughter was born. Again, I temporarily stopped debting, probably with the help of a Higher Power.

My parents' health started to become an issue. In 1981 my father had a massive stroke that left him paralyzed on his left side. My mother became his caregiver as well as his wife. In 1993 they moved into a brand new one-story condo so my mother could take care of my dad more easily. However, the same year my mother died unexpectedly in her sleep. It was a very sad time for all of us, especially my dad, and it left him paralyzed and in need of care.

Because my house was equipped to take care of a wheelchair patient, my dad came to live with us.

And so the stage was set for the next chapter—a man who needs me to take care of him, I am paying his bills, I have a history of debting and spending, but no program to deal with any of it. I would pay my dad's phone bill by writing a check to the phone company, then write a check to me; pay his cable bill and write a check to me. I felt I deserved it for taking care of him. I got good at signing his name. When one of those charge card applications came in the mail in his name, I signed it and sent it in. Got the card, and I was off again. In no time I had reached the limit of the card.

On any normal day my wife would get the mail and separate my father's bills from ours. For some reason (thank you, HP!) she opened the credit card statement for my father's card and saw the balance. I came home shortly afterward and she approached me with it. I denied it all the way: "I don't know how he charged all that; you know how he is, he likes to get stuff in the mail." She let it go. An hour later she asked me again, and I again denied it. Yet another half hour later she said that she really couldn't see how my father would charge so much, and she thought some of it was mine. I finally admitted to her that not only part of it, but all of it, was mine.

My wife was already in another Twelve-Step program and knew that my debting and spending was an addiction. She told me friends of hers were in a Twelve-Step program called Debtors Anonymous to help them with money issues, and that I should call them. I didn't want to, but I did. I called and asked if they could tell me more about D.A., and they said "coincidentally" they were going to a meeting that night. It must have been God's will, because on Tuesday, October 25, 1994, I went to my first D.A. meeting, and started on the road to recovery one day at a time.

I got a sponsor the next week and have been working with him ever since. My program today is continually working the Steps. I also participate in many PRGs and I work my spending plan to the best of my ability. Today I have a spiritual wealth that cannot be matched. I have acceptance as to where I am. I have balance in my life and of course I do service. Debtors Anonymous saved my life, and has taught me how to be an adult and how to fill the holes in my life with the important things in life, instead of the material things I used to use.

I am forever grateful to D.A. and to my Higher Power. I pray every day to do God's will, to walk down His path, not mine; to be the best husband, father, friend, and employee I can be; to be of service and to remember that God has led me this far and will not drop me now.

I know one day at a time that I can live a prosperous life, a fulfilled life, and a life of honor and dignity.

Thank you, D.A.!

Originally posted on the Debtors Anonymous website as "A One-time Liar and Cheat Finds a Life of Honor and Dignity."

28

Dependent on Plastic

A compulsive shopper breaks out of a family pattern of secrecy.

I am a compulsive spender and debtor in recovery. Two years ago I had $15,000 of credit-card debt. At that time my marriage was falling apart. My husband had always bailed me out before, but this time he said he was tired of being my "enabler" and he wouldn't come through for me again. He gave me six months to make radical changes in my life or our seven-year marriage was over. Fortunately for me and our two children, I took him seriously. I haven't used credit cards or incurred any new debt for more than two years, one day a time.

I grew up in the South in an upper-middle-class family. As long as I can remember, my parents argued about money. My mother would write checks and ring up her credit cards and expect my father to pick up the tab. It was obvious to my two older sisters and myself that our mother should discuss her purchases in advance with my father, rather than waiting for him to receive the bills and hit the roof. It was ironic that as an adult, I would find myself repeating the same pattern with my own husband.

Some of the messages about money that I learned as a child were:

- If you feel sad or depressed, go shopping and buy some new clothes. You will immediately (if temporarily) feel better.

- Don't worry if you can't afford to buy what you want immediately. Go ahead and buy it. There will always be someone to bail you out later.

- Keep your debts a secret.

Over the course of many years, my mother would secretly spend money she didn't really have. Then she'd try to hide the extent of the damage from my father. The best, or worst, example of my mother's secrecy about money was when my older sister was getting married and planned what I call a "pageant" wedding. My father had become blind before his death and needed my mother to pay the bills and manage their money.

My father had agreed to a budget of $7,000 for my sister's wedding. Our whole family thought it was fair. Years later, we learned that my mother had actually spent closer to $30,000 without my father's knowledge, or anyone else's for that matter. In hindsight, I think my sister would have preferred the cash. There were a few clues that my mom was overspending, like her paying for all ten bridesmaids' dresses and shoes, an expense ordinarily covered by the bridesmaids. Having a "spending plan" for the wedding and comparing budgeted to actual expenditures would have been a foreign concept to our family.

Before I became a grateful member of Debtors Anonymous, I had grown up to be surprisingly like my mother. I would go shopping when I was sad or angry, rather than expressing my true feelings directly, and I would rush each day to get to the mailbox so I could hide the credit card bills from my husband.

I always loved to shop at the large expensive department stores, still do, because the sales people are so solicitous. Never mind that they are motivated by the commissions they are hoping to make; the important thing is I feel pampered and respected. For someone who suffers from low self-esteem, it can be nice to hear a stranger say, "Oh, that looks great on you!" I would pretend I was a really wealthy person, and these purchases were just a trifle to me. It was great if the salesperson played along with my game, deferring to me in that certain way reserved for the rich and famous. I used to feel so important when I would open my wallet and choose a credit card from among the many I kept there. Even if I was using a credit card, I wanted everyone to know I had a gold card and would receive my platinum card in the mail any day. When I saw those credit cards lined up in my wallet, I felt rich and successful. I didn't feel I was enough without the plastic to show as proof of my worth. Poor people pay with cash, but rich people always charge everything, right? Wrong.

I remember when my debt was getting larger, and I had reached my limit on several credit cards. I had to remember my balances on each card to make sure I didn't present one that would be declined. It was getting a little stressful to go shopping. Guilt and shame were overwhelming as I would wait to hear if my credit card had been accepted. Strangely enough, I usually knew if I was close to my limit on each credit card and what my credit limits were, but I was often vague about the total amount of my debt and unclear about whether or not I could afford a particular purchase. It seemed worth it all, however, when I would leave department stores with new clothes wrapped in tissue and placed in shopping bags.

Once I got home with my purchases, I would try to slip the clothes into my closet without my husband noticing. I would cut off all the price tags immediately. Then I would slowly introduce different pieces of clothing throughout the next several weeks, always pretending these clothes had been in my closet all along, that I just hadn't worn them in awhile. I would do the same with my friends when they would compliment me on a purchase—I would pretend that I had bought it a long time ago, that they just had not seen it before.

Aside from my compulsive shopping, I would draft large sums of money from my credit cards to pay monthly bills. My husband and I had arbitrarily decided that $2,500 seemed like a lot of money, enough to cover most monthly expenses. So, when I didn't have enough money in my account to pay the telephone bill, for example, I would assume it was my fault. I would draft money from a credit card to pay the bill without my husband's knowledge. Once we were able to sit down and create a budget or spending plan together, we realized it actually cost closer to $5,000 per month to pay the bills for our family of four. I had been debting unnecessarily.

The worst part about using credit cards for me was when the bills came. I would rush to the mailbox each day to beat my husband, keeping him in the dark. After a while, he just assumed that I always collected and sorted the mail each day because I liked to. Little did he know how painful it really was. The reality of my overspending was there in black and white, plus 18% interest. I was usually able to pay only the minimum balance due.

Jung has said that "healing comes in relationship," and that has certainly been my experience. The biggest benefit of D.A. for me is just coming together week after week to be myself with other people who are willing to share themselves openly and honestly with the group. It is so important for me to be reminded that I am not alone.

Many people in D.A. have also said over the years, "We are only as guilty as our secrets." I have found this to be true. Confessing the full extent of my financial difficulties first to my husband, then to my therapist, and then to the members of my D.A. meeting were crucial steps in my healing process. It was important for me to say the exact amount of my debt and to be specific about how the money had been spent.

Another important action for me was cutting up all my credit cards. Six months before I had "bottomed out," I cut up all my cards except one. I rationalized that since the bill had to be paid within thirty days, I couldn't get into serious debt. The reality was that I would overspend on my credit card and borrow from other sources to make payments. I have come to realize that if I don't have enough cash to buy something, then I can't afford it. Also, if I consider buying something that costs over $100, I need to discuss it first with my husband. Even if he agrees, however, I have learned it is important for me to wait twenty-four hours before making a major purchase. Then I can feel good about what I buy and not worry that I have bought something compulsively.

Letting go of that last card was symbolic for me. It meant I no longer needed to get my sense of self-worth from a piece of plastic. It meant I would live within my means each month and not have a crutch to fall back on. It meant I was ready to act like a "grown-up" and take responsibility for my financial life.

To commemorate my graduation from credit cards, I took the cut-up pieces and made them into a collage. On the left side of my collage is a man surrounded by credit cards and drowning in a can of tomato soup. On the right side of the collage is a tribute to "honesty and willingness." Included are pictures of what my Higher Power has come to represent for me, such as a mountain for strength, a whale for depth. These qualities are not outside of me, but I now realize are hidden within.

I also have a picture of Beauty and the Beast in my collage. For years, I lived a life of quiet desperation. I have always been a people pleaser, learning at an early age to discern what others want and need, often without regard for my own needs or desires. It was important that I appear competent and perfect, because I felt so unworthy and inadequate. I am still afraid sometimes that if I show my true self, complete with imperfections, no one could really love or respect me. As I strived for perfection and presented a managed personality, a beast inside me would periodically flare up and express itself through my compulsive spending and debting. Not until I was willing to face that beast and admit to being only human was I able to get a sense of who I really am. I am just beginning to learn what I want and need for the first time in my life. By facing the beast, it can be transformed into something really interesting and beautiful.

When I first came to D.A., I wasn't sure I had anything in common with most of the people in the room. I wanted to get rid of my affliction, get out of debt, and move on as soon as possible. Now, I am completely out of debt and record my expenses every day. I understand now what people mean when they say D.A. is not really about the money. Getting my finances in order is only one piece of the program. In a way, solvency is a mere side effect of working the Twelve Steps and realizing the spiritual implications of being a debtor. I now know I have something in common with every person who attends a D.A. meeting, regardless of their financial situation. The beast within me will always be there, but it is out of the shadows of denial and secrecy. The light of awareness has permanently altered the landscape of my life, and I will forever be grateful.

By the way, I still love shopping and the smell of new clothes, but now I feel fantastic when I buy something I can afford and pay cash. Keep coming back. It works!

Originally published in the first edition of *A Currency of Hope.*

29

Loving as Money; Money as Love

Money became her measure for love, and finally her lover.
In D.A. she learned to be present as a businesswoman, mother, and wife.

I became obsessed with money when I was in the fourth grade. I asked my grandmother for "just a little" so I could go downtown to buy myself "a little something." It was as much my quick fix then as it became for me later as an adult.

Money in my pocket gave me something to do so I didn't have to see my loneliness, sit with it, or remain alone with it. Buying something gave me somewhere important to go, and with a rush of adrenaline and a feeling of excitement, I became worthwhile (for a little while) as I purchased my gift for the day. When I was given money, I was loved, simple as that. And knowing I could somehow always "get it" gave me a feeling of power and superiority that just turned out to be other words for egocentricity. It never made me feel good for very long. Then I'd ask for more money. I didn't get what I needed. Instead of getting love, I only got a feeling of control and an ability to "act out."

As a teen, looking good meant being wanted and admired. I was voted Best Dressed of the Senior Class. The school photographer took a picture of me all dressed up looking in the mirror at myself. The reflection of those sad baby-blue eyes and a ghost of a smile pasted on my face always reminded me of that Peggy Lee song "Is That All There Is?"

I got married the summer after graduation, depressed and desperately lonely, and loving his large close-knit family and wanting company. I knew he'd be a good father and a hard worker, and he'd help me belong and fit in. And yes, look good.

We bought several homes and each time, I would start a major home improvement plan. I'd already changed complete living room furnishings several times. I would tire of them after several months and call the store, finding something wrong with them so they'd take them back. I always used credit, so I mostly got my way. Meanwhile, I wasn't very available to my children, not having much time for them, so driven I was by things. I was in love with those things. I really believed that if my home looked good enough, people would want me. I wouldn't be alone.

After five homes, including lots of moving and marriage problems, my husband and I decided to start our own house-building business. I had a hard time staying in our home office handling customer calls, because we were bringing in a lot of money, and I wanted to spend it. We usually received one-half of the down payment for the homes up front. I saw it as mine and spendable. I talked our landholder into releasing part of our business property acreage to build a model home on. Then, the bank didn't require any down payment and gave us a full construction loan. I felt very clever and smug about pulling this off; I had no idea how we'd pay for that mortgage.

Soon it was clear my marriage was breaking up. I hardly had time for intimacy because I was so preoccupied with money. Somehow I had married a man who left me alone a lot, and money became my lover.

When I finally got the courage to look at our financial state and my marriage state, I decided to go, leaving it all for him. I figured he hadn't loved or wanted me, so he could have the bills. He soon had to file for bankruptcy, and our new model house was repossessed. I was on my way to another marriage, so it didn't take long for the old marriage to be a complete disaster. We simply moved, and ran up bills, and moved again. Finally we divorced, and I found myself in a little studio apartment. My children lived with their father. I had a table, rocker, and a mattress on the floor I bought for $2 at a garage sale. I had trouble staying at any one job. I would get tired and hopeless, just barely surviving and living like a pauper. Usually I picked jobs that were unhealthy for me, acting out or getting fired. I thought they too owed me, and when they tired of my taking time off, rearranging my work schedule, or just play-ing, the job would end.

I finally landed a job where I was able to perform and earned a pretty good salary. I became fairly stable. I met my husband-to-be and moved to suburbia in an affluent area of town. He had a nice home, but it needed attention. Once again, without even seeing it, I went on a rampage of decorating and shopping and spending. But this time, because I was married to a man with a stable job and excellent credit history, I had credit cards! I can still remember how I felt when one of the salespeople at a department store called me by name after she rang up a sale, saying "Thank you, Mrs. _____."

I felt such a rush of importance and respect. I was finally fitting in with the rest of the community. I had buying power! I had a lovely home, my children were now with me, and I had a job where I was considered "the hub of the wheel," and a good salary: quite a respectable life. I felt so loved and admired.

After we financed our home a second time, using all our equity to pay off credit cards, we just spent up to our credit limit. Once again, I knew I was in trouble.

I started lying about my income. I acquired four major credit cards with high limits. Now I became really depressed. I was actually afraid to leave the house to go to work, because I'd been away from work for so long. I felt more and more isolated, more and more alone. I didn't want to see friends, because I couldn't look good anymore, and because even I didn't believe my big plans and schemes. My self-will and brainstorming for all these months had not worked, and now I was so afraid that I couldn't even think. Several months before coming to Debtors Anonymous, I realized I was doing some very sick and wrong things, and I had the feeling something was coming to an end. I thought it might be my life.

First, I took money from an investment account of my daughter's that was paid her from an accident settlement as a result of a drunk driver. Four hundred dollars had not yet been invested, and without her permission I asked for the check to be sent to me. I did not tell her, but just kept thinking and hoping I'd replace it. Finally, when school was about to begin, I charged her school clothes. I told her that instead of her using her money, I would deduct her clothes from what I owed her. It became so complicated that I finally broke down one afternoon and told her what I had really done and how bad I felt, mostly about how it felt to need money from my twelve-year-old daughter.

Next were the sad instances of the gift certificates. I charged certificates at two different department stores, for $50 each, in my daughter's name. I asked them if she get could get the cash back, if she didn't find anything, and the answer was yes. When I took my daughter with me to get the money, both stores made a big stink, saying she'd have to purchase something. We bought socks, and they refunded us the rest. All this for $90 cash and more debting. Worse, I was role modeling for my daughter how to charge, how to debt, and how to do something dishonest. Lucky her, for being the one to sign the certificates.

When I got to Debtors Anonymous, it was a Tuesday night in August 1992, the worst night of my life, I thought. I didn't say a word, hardly looking at anyone. I have never felt so shameful and so afraid. If I had tried to talk, I knew I would cry. I cried afterward all the way home. I did hear the suggestion of eight meetings in the next six weeks and to keep coming back. I did, too, attending two meetings a week, consistently. I took to heart the idea of keeping a spending record, and I did for the next two months. By the third meeting, I had accepted a new half-time position in a good place, with good folks. By the grace of God, it was just in time for me. By the fourth meeting, my husband came along. I heard him say he was afraid that things had gotten so bad that our relationship might not survive and that he hoped these meetings would "help me." I was amazed he had even spoken to a roomful of strangers, especially about our troubled marriage. I was really frightened, and it hit me that we were in deep trouble.

Then the weekend came, and all our kids were home. I got up early and went shopping. Hours later, I found myself in the dressing room at a department store shaking and sweating, thinking that I could not get out of this place and that I might have to have the saleswoman call my husband. I felt immobilized, unable to make a decision. I thought about how much I was missing at home, how this would have been a good time to talk to my son, and how I had wanted to see all of them, but now the day was half over. I finally got to my car and drove home, leaving my packages in the car to sneak in later. I had gone to the grocery store before I got home so I could say I was grocery shopping and doing "a few errands," my line for lying about shopping. Kinda like having "just a few drinks." When I got home I felt sick and went to bed, where I cried so hard and long that I finally called for help. I called someone in the program. Luckily, he was calm and accepting, saying it sounded like I had gone out to try one last time and gotten the shakes, so I probably had reached bottom and really scared myself. He suggested that I pray and read Step One. I never thought I would be totally reliant on Step One, but now I was willing to do anything. I knew I was powerless over my spending and debting, and that only a Power greater than myself could help me now. Somehow I had believed my friend who had to get to Step One in order to stop drinking, but I didn't think I would ever be so out of control with my "silly ol' spending." That afternoon I made the decision to turn my life and my will over to the care of God. And I got out of bed!

Within two weeks my husband and I had our first Pressure Relief Group. Things looked bleak and hopeless, and I thought there were probably no choices. But for the first time, everything was down on paper, and reality was pretty clear. We listed a homework and action plan and scheduled our new Pressure Relief Group. It appeared we all felt better. I made my ideal wish list spending plan, writing down all my expenditures. I loved that part. Then I wrote my dream salary. Of course when I added it all up, I had overspent by $22,000. Even with an income of $100,000 a year, I was still short. Finally the disease had begun to speak to me!

Our next Pressure Relief Group was with a married couple, both in our program. My husband was skeptical, believing this program was great for my spending problem, but he didn't see why he needed it. He was concerned only with paying bills, that was all. The issue of trust arose, and I realized the reason we had separate checking accounts might have something to do with trust and secrets.

I was thankful for both of them taking responsibility for their joint debting, spending, and pauper problems. Obviously this was not about just one person.

I learned about my spending and how when I felt deprived, or when my basic needs came last, after bill paying, I became compulsive and angry. I came to realize that looking good to hide feeling bad had never worked. It had never made me OK with myself, or lovable. I found that in my "terminal vagueness," I hadn't even known what my own business really made, though it was my business earnings that qualified us for a low-interest home loan, saving us money on our mortgage and greatly reducing our debt load.

In early December we went to an all-cash spending plan. Our best gift was a Christmas without credit. The day after Christmas, we looked at each other and smiled, knowing we owed no one anything and with the peace of mind that this was the right road now.

I had hoped we could be one of those program couples who could make a new life, forgive, and build new trust with our commitment to the program. But this is a dangerous, rampant, insidious disease that can kill, and sometimes there is too much damage and denial until it's too late.

Miracles happen. And this program works. It may not work the way we planned it or dreamed it, but the folks in the meetings and Pressure Relief Groups are messengers in the spirit of this lifesaving and life-changing program. Now I have support and friendship, love and intimacy, and a new family in this program. I can now make proactive choices for growth and happiness for myself and my daughter, moving ahead to how I want to live my life. Today, instead of pretending and looking good to fit in so my family will love me, I am living openly, according to my true nature. Somehow, when I stopped hiding and being vague around money issues, I became clear about other areas of my life. Instead of acting out the ugly duckling I believed I was, I found that a beautiful swan had been there all along—strength, courage, and all.

If the saying "You have to lose a life to gain a life" is true, then I thank God for my new life.

Originally published in the first edition of *A Currency of Hope.*

⁓

30

Recovery in New Hampshire

*D.A. was forty miles away, but it helped so much
that this debtor brought it home.*

Debtors Anonymous is the most gut-wrenching program I've ever en-
countered. At the same time, it offers hope and recovery from compulsive debting. It has forced me to examine hopes, dreams, fears, and old beliefs,
many of them well hidden under a feast/famine mentality that I didn't even
know I had.

When I came into D.A. eleven months ago, I was in pain and hopeless,
buried under about $101,500 of secured and unsecured debt. At the outset,
the vicious cycle of borrowing and repayment had seemed perfectly logical.
Cash flow for my business had declined, and I had thousands of dollars of
credit in bank credit lines and credit cards of every description and color,
including gold, silver, and platinum. I knew I was trustworthy and solvent, or
these people wouldn't have advanced me this much credit. And that started
the downward slide into ever-deepening debt, depression, and fear; the worse
it became, the more I debted, until at the end I was practically immobilized.

For quite a while I hid, ostrich-like. The higher and higher levels of debt
weren't due to department store spending or indulging myself in extravaganc-
es. In fact, when I hit bottom, only one department store card was affected.
The debts were due to the attempt to keep my business afloat, marred con-
siderably by an ego-driven business decision that cost plenty in money and

forced me to really examine my egocentricity. Why else would one engage in a problematic business venture with a glib, little-known business partner and no business plan? Since my mounting debt wasn't for "goodies" for myself, I rationalized that it really didn't count. There would always be one more credit card to borrow from, cash flow would improve, the "big fix" would happen, and miraculously I would be saved.

This eventually came to a screeching halt. I was facing thousands of dollars of payments due or past due, with a cash flow at subsistence level, and creditors beginning to hound my every waking hour. It was then I found D.A. And it was then I made the inner commitment not to debt, no matter what, one day at a time.

The journey into recovery has been slow and decidedly erratic. I wish I could state that by following my decision, cash flow improved. That I made steady progress in paying off indebtedness, and that I've built significant cash reserves. None of that is true.

What did happen is that I cancelled credit cards and contacted all my creditors (a painful process), but I was getting threatening, harassing, and intimidating phone calls from almost all of them. My cash flow remained very low. Even putting my own needs first—bare bones needs like paying rent and food—has been a daily struggle. Frequently, I had to juggle a car payment with money for the phone bill, robbing Peter to pay Paul.

That is the downside, but I have had many positives. My primary benefit so far has been that no matter what happened, I didn't debt one day at a time. Sometimes it was agonizingly painful, but I did learn. I learned how to participate in my own recovery. I work the program constantly. I keep spending records, spending plans, and creditor contact logs. By recording my contacts with creditors, I discovered they often misrepresented what I had told them, or told me I had promised something I hadn't. Eventually I stopped phone contacts altogether and now insist on having all communication in writing. The more I took these steps, the more I realized my own power. It became clear to me that by my commitment to repay every cent I owe, I wasn't the "bad" or "deadbeat" person these collection people were addressing. This changed the tenor of our conversations. I learned, too, that their threats were just that, threats. If they had the power and authority they claimed, they wouldn't resort to intimidation. I learned to respond calmly in the face of their anger.

As frequently as possible I attend D.A. meetings. This isn't easy, because I live and work in a place where the closest meetings used to be about forty miles away. Attending meetings might have cost me in time and gas, but making the effort was participating in my own recovery.

What became clear was that I needed support in my own area, and that led to a significant step in my recovery: starting new meetings. I attended Intergroup meetings to learn how, and then started a D.A. group in my home town. Working independently, another person started a group in a town about twenty minutes away. We now work together supporting each other's meetings, giving Pressure Relief Groups, and trying to build D.A. in the state. I did the best I could. I found a meeting place, put signs in shops around town, put a notice in our community newspaper, and showed up week after week, no matter what. Currently attendance at our meetings is growing, so the word about D.A. is getting out.

Finally, I began working on some of my more gut-wrenching issues. I realized that I had spent most of my life in the feast/famine cycle, going from no debt to increasingly huge debt, paying it off and starting over. There is still an active part of me that wants to continue this, but my commitment to the program is such that I no longer have to do this. Sometimes it is a struggle because the destructive part of me and my compulsive behaviors are still very much alive.

I looked at my spending and realized that the cause—whether I was borrowing to float my business or charging at clothiers to dress nicely—didn't matter. My spending and debting were way out of proportion to reality. As one of my gifts of D.A., I came to realize that I could begin to balance income with outgo. Much of my spending had been "fix it," with "it" being anything from a disturbing encounter that day to my entire life. I used spending and debting to feel better, to appear grown-up and in control, and to make myself OK. All of these are addressed in D.A. Now I don't have to do those things. I can step back, think, and walk through uncomfortable feelings without debting.

With almost a year in D.A., even with a greatly reduced cash flow, I have reduced my debt to about $88,500. While that's a significant reduction, I still have a long way to go. But what I didn't understand when I first came into D.A. is that money is not the issue. What matters is the strength and recovery

I have. I've learned that owing money doesn't make me a bad person. I've learned that in a business transaction they want their money, and I want to pay them. All we are discussing is how.

D.A. has given me back some control over my life and my finances. I've learned to stay positive, not to give in to the doubt and despair that comes with this compulsive disease. I've learned I do have a compulsive disease, but with the help of D.A. and my Higher Power, I can be healed. Thank you, D.A. Thank you, God.

Originally published in the first edition of *A Currency of Hope*.

31

The Gift of Awareness

*Though driven into D.A. with negative net worth
and a bad car loan, she found miracles.*

My compulsive debting dates back to getting my first credit card. My first year in graduate school was also my first experience of supporting myself through my own contributions. Although my salary was $411 a month, I saved $1,786 in ten months—enough to buy my first car. Then I got my first credit card, because I heard you needed it to establish a credit rating. I began with a $100 credit limit. Ten years later, I had four credit cards maxed out to $6,000 of unsecured debt. Interesting, how that happened. Every year around Christmas, I could count on a $200 raise in credit limit from at least one credit card. Each time, I'd swear up and down that I wouldn't use the credit, but I was always maxed out again by the next April. I always got a "raise" from the credit card companies, because I made debt repayment Number One on my priority list. If it came to a choice between going to the dentist or keeping current with my credit cards, guess which one I chose?

Because I was never hounded by irate creditors, it was easy for me to deny a problem. The issue that bottomed me out was an open-end car lease I took on when I got my first "real" job out of graduate school. The car had to be worth a given amount at the end of the lease. If it wasn't, I would make up the difference. I felt uneasy about entering the lease, because I worried that I couldn't take good enough care of the car for it to be at the desired value at the end of the lease. The car wasn't even what I wanted. I was taking over a lease on a car with 15,000 miles on it. My boyfriend had set the deal up through a buddy. All my instincts told me to wait for a better deal. Bur in the spirit of "terminal vagueness" that typifies my compulsive debting, I signed the lease contract anyway.

My instincts proved to be right. I discovered my lease had all the disadvantages of actual car ownership with none of the advantages. I discovered that to renew the car registration, I had to pay an old parking ticket from the previous lessor. The car also had "little" things wrong: doors that wouldn't unlock, the rear trunk lid flew open without warning, and numerous other problems. I was determined to get rid of the car at the lease end, but was worried sick it wouldn't be worth its true value.

About a year into the lease, I started recovering in Overeaters Anonymous. Six months into my O.A. recovery, however, I started noticing things about my spending. I realized that though my salary was a lot bigger than in graduate school, I still didn't have enough money. A brochure from a bank showed how to calculate net worth, and to my dismay, mine was negative! The outcome of the car lease threatened to take my net worth even further down. What was wrong?

As the end of the lease drew near, I told my O.A. sponsor my fears of owing more to the leasing company than I could pay. She told me about Debtors Anonymous and referred me to a woman who took me to my first D.A. meeting. At first I wasn't sure whether I qualified. After all, I thought, I can pay my bills, so did I really belong with all those people who couldn't? But I was so scared about that lease, I stayed and did everything they told me.

I started writing my money down and had a Pressure Relief Meeting after three months. One member of my Pressure Relief Group pointed out that for the monthly $200 I was paying for the leased car, I could have had a brand-new car. I was very angry, because I felt I'd been taken advantage of. My anger inspired me to do the right thing in the wrong way: without consulting my Pressure Relief Group, I bought a new car using the leased car as the trade-in. Typically, I did not get clarity on the value of the leased car before I bought the new one. It was a big surprise the next month when a letter from the leasing company informed me that the discrepancy between what the car was supposed to be worth and how they valued it was $2,348! After reading that letter, I got down on my knees and prayed. With the help of my Pressure Relief Group, I negotiated a settlement for $1,100 that I was able to pay off—in cash—only nine months after my first D.A. meeting. How did this miracle happen, when I'd never had more than a hundred or two in savings? I'm not sure. In D.A., all I did was write my money down and not debt, one day at a time. Suddenly, I had money in the bank.

That was the first miracle that Debtors Anonymous worked in my life. I'm very grateful to D.A. and to my Higher Power for extracting me from the mess I'd gotten myself into. The biggest difference in my life since then is that I've been able to use the tool of awareness so that I can avoid situations like the car lease in the first place.

You don't hear much about awareness in D.A., so I'd like to make a pitch for it here. If you've ever read the A.A. "Big Book," you may be familiar with the chapter called "More About Alcoholism." That chapter gives many examples of "alcoholic thinking," that is, the lame excuses that alcoholics give for drinking. The only freedom from alcoholic thinking must come from a Higher Power. As a compulsive debtor, I identified with the "alcoholic thinking" in my own disease, because I saw that "debting thinking" got me into the car lease mess. My main defense against "debting thinking" has been awareness. For me, awareness is not just a tool of the D.A. program; I see it as both a tool and a result of working the Twelve Steps—a gift from my Higher Power. Awareness is that little voice from my Higher Power that counteracts "debting thinking." Two examples from my later D.A. recovery illustrate this:

I signed up for a ballroom dance class with a famous dance studio. After I completed my first six lessons, I wanted to take more. However, the dance studio kept pressuring me to sign up for $3,200 worth of lessons "on time." Because of the gift of awareness, the unsecured debt immediately raised a red flag. I resisted their efforts to get me to sign up for a large number of lessons and arranged to take lessons on a pay-as-you-go basis. After taking a few lessons that way, I realized I wasn't making any progress. They wouldn't accommodate my needs; they wanted to pressure me into all the lessons at once and then map out a program for me. As weeks went by, I realized too that most people weren't there to learn how to dance. It was more of a social club. So, I quit.

I admit I didn't do this perfectly. The "Love Myself" savings fund suggested by my Pressure Relief Group was $800 poorer. I probably would have spent even less of my fund if I'd kept in better contact with my Pressure Relief Group. However, the gift of awareness undoubtedly saved me from incurring $3,200 in unsecured debt. In that sense, the $800 was money well spent. Progress, not perfection.

With the support of my Pressure Relief Group, I asked my credit card companies to cancel my line of credit. I could no longer use the cards, but I still received monthly statements and made payments. About a year later, a letter from one credit card company offered $5 if I reopened my line of credit. My debting mentality jumped at the thought: "Wow! Sounds like an easy $5. They must be counting on my using the credit line so they can get the interest, but if I just reactivate the account without charging, I'll get the $5." I felt a funny twinge of awareness: I racked my brain trying to figure out why the bank would want to give me $5. I soon realized it was the $18 annual service fee. I'd be incurring $13 in unsecured debt: the $18 service fee minus the $5 for reactivating my account. Bully for awareness for warning me. This time around took only fifteen minutes to see the "catch."

This all shows me that just because I've paid off my debts doesn't mean I'm "cured." I'll always need awareness, the gift from my Higher Power, to protect me from making financial decisions not in my best interest.

Originally published in the first edition of *A Currency of Hope*.

32

"Scarlett" Comes Home to D.A.

A drama queen took debting to the limit and found Higher Power.

I spent my entire life living beyond my means. As I child I had dreamed of a Scarlett O'Hara–like existence. As an adult I tried to make this dream a reality. I employed cleaning ladies, serving women for parties, housekeepers, and nannies. I served the best food and liquor money could buy. I shopped at the most expensive stores for my children's clothes and mine and vacationed around the world. How could I do this on my husband's construction worker salary, you ask? It was easy: Beg, borrow, or steal. And when that didn't work, there were always credit cards. My theme song was "Take me to the limit one more time." I managed to squander both my husband's and my salary on looking good, but it wasn't long before all my money and marriage were "Gone with the Wind."

After leaving my family and moving to California, I was faced with the truth. I was a debtor, a pauper, and an underachiever. Oh, don't get me wrong. I could make lots of money, but I couldn't hold onto it. My family stopped bailing me out when time after time I ran another credit card to the limit. I came to a crashing halt. I had to live within my means. There was no place else to turn. Depression and suicidal thoughts were with me constantly. Now my bills were double my earnings, and I realized I would soon be living on the street.

Though I didn't know about D.A., I did start working the Steps in another program. Many people were encouraging me to go on Social Security, because I could barely work. I decided to try to support myself as best I could. It was the first time I had taken responsibility for myself, and it felt good. As part of my Fourth Step, I did financial amends, paying off all my credit cards and most of my debts. I was earning more money, and I had the feeling I could conquer the world.

That summer my uncle died, and I was left a large sum of money. I was made trustee for my children's and my widowed aunt's money. It was money, money, money, money that brought me to D.A. six months later. I was again depressed, suicidal, and hysterical. I felt totally responsible and afraid I would make a mistake and lose all the money. I tried to hide, manipulate, and control everyone's funds. I got greedy and wanted more, so I would feel secure. But no matter how I hoarded, counted, or concealed it, there just was not enough. I look back on these months as my Silas Marner period. I had no life, no God—just money. My relationship with my children was based on money. It was all we talked about: They asked for it, and I was the "Almighty" that decided whether they could have it. I was sick, hysterical, and unsure of my life, but completely in control of theirs. How could this be happening when I had worked the Steps and was in a Twelve-Step program for over ten years?

On New Year's Day eight years ago, I joined D.A. I went to a meeting every week. I set up a Pressure Relief Group immediately and have met with the same two people almost every month since joining D.A. Thanks to the commitment of this man and woman, I have lost many of my fears. I have gone from boxes of bills, papers, and twelve bankbooks to one Higher Power. I went from depending on my will to surrendering to God's. One of the most difficult issues I faced was using money from savings for my everyday life. Every time I dipped into savings for food and shelter, I faced my deprivation issues. I wanted to save the money or hide it, but never to spend it. I was afraid if I spent it, there wouldn't be enough. Some people in the program think their problems would be solved by a certain sum of money. I have not found that to be true. Even today, I call on my Higher Power when using prudent reserve funds or savings. I remind myself that there is enough. I am being taken care of by my HP.

Money is no longer my god. I turned my children's money over to them after educating them on how to manage it. They make mistakes, but that's

how they learn. I trust that they have an HP, too. My relationship is clear
with all in my family, thanks to D.A. I have learned money is only a tool. I
am financially solvent and earn more now than in the past seven years. The
most important thing I have received from D.A. is the personal relationship I
have with my Higher Power. All the meetings, literature, phone calls, Pressure
Relief Groups, and sponsors have only one purpose: to help you and me find
God. My HP is right here when I am in need. No matter how much or how
little money I have, I'm OK. I have enough, because I am enough. Thanks to
D.A., I don't have to cling to the mud of Tara to keep me safe. I am at home,
no matter where I am. D.A. is my home.

Originally published in the first edition of *A Currency of Hope* as "Scarlett Comes Home to D.A."

33

Mario's Story

*With the support of the Fellowship, he stayed solvent
throughout his fatal illness.*

This year, I celebrate four years of recovery in Debtors Anonymous. Five years ago, I decided that the reason I felt so hopeless around money was that I hadn't applied myself. Well, after one year of applying my self-knowledge, I was even more hopeless than when I began. I was ready for help. Now I was teachable, and my Higher Power brought me to my first D.A. meeting. I had many years' experience in other Twelve-Step programs, so it was a little easier to fit in. Still, I walked in with much fear, shame, and confusion about my finances. My love interest had been going to D.A. for a year, and his life seemed to be improving, especially around his finances. He didn't once suggest I go to D.A., but as the program says, it is attraction rather than promotion.

Well, it worked. My partner drove helpless me to my first D.A. meeting on a bleak December Sunday, and I'll always be grateful for the principles of Debtors Anonymous. I hated my first year of meetings, but I knew I was in the right place. I kept coming back.

I've never had open-heart surgery, but I think I now know what it feels like. When other members shared about not being able to buy underwear, not opening mail, feeling like there wasn't enough, like they weren't enough, not knowing how to deal with creditors, I felt I wasn't alone. That feeling of hopelessness I had learned to accommodate was lifted at my first meeting and has not returned. That's one of the most precious gifts I've received from D.A.

A lot of my recovery has focused on the fact that I live with another life-threatening disease besides debting, though I have seen debting kill people as cunningly as drugs or alcohol. I am a recovering debtor who is living with AIDS. As my recovery progresses, so does the AIDS virus. I'm learning that just as I am powerless over debting and cannot recover alone, neither can I deal with AIDS by myself. As an active debtor, I became isolated and secretive. So it's a miracle of D.A. that last night I had a D.A. meeting in my home with an oxygen tube in my nose and six other D.A. members who have helped me in more ways than they'll ever know. I hope I've helped them; that's how it works!

When I came to D.A., I knew I had to eventually do service, if I were going to stay. I made coffee, became the literature person, gave my phone number to newcomers (even though I felt I had nothing to offer), gave and received Pressure Relief Groups, and became a part of Intergroup. The effort I've put into my program has come back to me tenfold in the way of friendships, serenity, self-esteem, and self-love.

One painful and joyful lesson I keep learning in D.A. is that I have needs, and they all deserve to be met. As I grew up in a family of debtors, having a need was just unheard of. As a debtor living—and I emphasize living—with AIDS, I have many needs. When my virus is causing me to feel sick, my first instinct is to hoard all my resources and shut down. That is my disease rearing its ugly head. I've tasted enough abundance to not stay there for very long, and I actively use the tools of D.A. That's a miracle—getting out of being stuck, shut down. That was how I lived twenty-four hours a day, before D.A.

Because of the Twelve Steps and principles of D.A. and its loving members, I've maintained my health insurance, stayed solvent even with my medical bills, and received massages, affection, and physical and emotional support. I feel loved and supported by my Higher Power and all of my needs are being met. I'm able to open my mail daily. I'm in a loving relationship with the debtor who Twelve-Stepped me—we just celebrated six years. I pay for my therapy weekly, and I could go on and on. You get the picture, though.

I have not had a perfect recovery, although I would like to. My smart-mouthed therapist referred to me as "little Gandhi." OK, I get it! I have not had a formal sponsor for two years, and I don't think I've ever completed any of my Action Plans, and I've not been treasurer, but this is all OK; I am enough.

Especially to anyone new to D.A.: I hope I've given you a message of hope. I've learned through D.A. that no suffering member is hopeless—I'm proof of that.

When I came to D.A. in December, I didn't have enough money to buy a gift. As I celebrate my fourth year in D.A., I just made a list of presents I'm buying (my name is at the top), and we are planning a Christmas party that's within each other's spending plan. The best present I get every December is that I am a member of Debtors Anonymous.

Publisher's note: This member died on December 4, 1992.

Originally published in the first edition of *A Currency of Hope.*

34

Caring for Myself

Though his early family experiences taught him shame,
he learned to value himself in D.A.

As a recovering member of Debtors Anonymous for over five years, I have achieved clarity about what it means to care for myself In D.A., I have learned to sort through the various manifestations of the disease and to identify with others. Although my story is simple, it also reveals ways of manifesting the disease of compulsive debting that I thought of as unique to me.

My first debt was to my parents, and I incurred it when I was only seven or eight years old. I received an allowance, and I was supposed to set a portion aside to pay for school supplies in September. Being a kid, however, what I really wanted was to buy baseball cards, like the other boys could. When school started, I had no money for pencils and notebooks.

My mother and I made an agreement that, instead of receiving a nickel for drying the dinner dishes, that money would be used to pay down my debt. I can still remember the shame I felt and the fear I had that this debt would *never* be paid off. I had the sense that I could not hold my head up as long as I owed that money.

Years later, I've come to see that, while it was simply my parents' intention to teach me responsibility about money, I was too young for such a lesson.

What I took away from that experience instead was a sense that I was incapable of managing money or of supporting myself.

Over the years, I lived with my sense of inadequacy. Although my background was comfortably middle-class and we didn't lack anything material, even with my parents' conservative tastes, I lived in fear of being without income.

Despite my fears of not being able to take care of myself, I acquired a profession and a career in civil service. Having grown up New York City, I took advantage of my new status to relocate, first to Washington, D.C., then to San Francisco.

I started to acquire credit cards and with each, soon charged up to the limit. I would go into a panic and focus all my effort toward paying them off as quickly as possible to avoid the shame of my childhood debting experiences. In keeping with that, I put the needs of my creditors before my own, reinforcing the idea that I needed to pay them off to be an acceptable human being.

I came to my first D.A. meeting more than ten years ago. At that time, I was earning more money than I ever had before. Yet each week my money dwindled away more quickly. I had recently returned to San Francisco from a trip to a wedding on the East Coast. Transportation, lodging, and the wedding gift I charged to my credit card, because I didn't have any cash. Shortly after moving to San Francisco, I had purchased a late-model used car and had left all the details of financing and insurance up to the car dealer. I was vague about what it would cost me for loan payments and insurance, and since I hadn't planned on buying a car, I hadn't allowed for the expense of keeping it. Nor had I found a place to live where I could park a car off-street. I found myself paying, in addition to my rent, a monthly fee for garage space.

In order to generate enough cash for all these unplanned expenses, I purposely had an inadequate amount of money withheld from my paycheck for income taxes. I had no idea what I would do when the time came the following year.

By the time I reached D.A., I had cleaned up other areas of my life in other Twelve-Step programs. I knew the Steps worked, but I couldn't conceive of how to apply them to my money problems. What I did know was that I couldn't control my situation. While my debts were relatively modest in dollars compared to some of the stories I heard in my early meetings, they were more than I could deal with on my own.

I went to meetings, listened, and told my new friends in D.A. what was going on with me. Despite my fears of disclosing my financial situation to others, I quickly assembled a Pressure Relief Group. My previous money difficulties and my acquaintance with some of the early D.A. members in Washington, D.C. had motivated me to start keeping spending records.

My Pressure Relief Group showed me I could make sound choices in order to get my needs met. They assured me that, if I wanted to, I could keep my car. They worked with me while I searched for a new apartment that would meet my needs better and still cost a great deal less than the previous one. They held my hand as I got clarity about my tax situation. Later on, my Pressure Relief Group and my other D.A. friends supported me in the painful process of dealing with my debt to the IRS. The job I moved to San Francisco to take was not suited for me. Working the Third Step, I requested reassignment and was able to stay in the same office, with no decrease in pay.

My recovery in D.A. helped me to form and maintain an abundant and rewarding relationship with a loving partner, who followed me into D.A. (and whose story also appears in these pages). As I write these words, I mourn his passing from AIDS, an event which happened just a few weeks ago. Thanks to this program working in both our lives, we were able to share a beautiful home for the final two years of his life. Each of us, with the help and support of our program, was able to plan vacations beyond what we ever could have conceived prior to recovery—all paid for, in cash, without depriving ourselves in other areas.

It is a tribute to this D.A. recovery that my partner had adequate medical care, and there was no financial crisis after he died. It is a signpost of my recovery that I could have provided financial support, if it had been necessary. In addition, during the process of his dying, it was important that I get my needs met so that I could be there for him. It took all the resources I could muster from my recovery to ask for help, to ask for time away from him, to allow myself opportunities for fun and recreation so that I could be emotionally available for him and for myself.

It is hard to conceive of anything more painful than the loss of a loved one from a terminal illness. I know that I too am at risk for AIDS, and this fact is an important part of my D.A. program. It means that health care is a high priority in my spending plan; my physical, spiritual, and emotional well-being come first in my life. It also gives me the humility I need to live my life one day at a time.

I've long since paid off my unsecured debts, including my debt to the IRS. Those were the debts that brought me to my knees and brought me to the rooms of Debtors Anonymous. Even my car loan has been paid off. The money my Higher Power brings into my life is mine to use as I see fit: to meet all of my needs and many of my desires, to contribute to the causes I care about, and to give myself a prudent reserve.

As I look to the future, I know that my continued well-being depends upon my willingness to continue to reach out for support and for love. First and foremost, I must ask for the help of my Higher Power on a daily basis. That spiritual support is, after all, the very foundation of the D.A. program. In addition, I have always to reach out to my friends in D.A. and to all of the resources, which I am now able to believe I deserve. I am worthy.

Originally published in the first edition of *A Currency of Hope.*

35

Financial Fantasy Gives Way to Bright Reality

He finds the gift of clarity through the Twelve Steps.

I was always a deeply sensitive and imaginative child who, under the stress of my family's long-term poverty, retreated into a perpetual pink, fuzzy haze of fantasy and daydreams, a pint-size Walter Mitty.

My devoted and hardworking mother, Rachel, did her best to raise and support ten children, seven of whom survived to adulthood. In the Depression we lost our large farm in Connecticut and ended up on public assistance, with my Dad working for the Works Progress Administration on construction projects. There was very often a shortage of money for rent and clothing (except shoes), but never a lack of delicious, healthful food in plentiful amounts, as Mama was a gourmet cook who could feed ten people on two chickens and a salad!

My childhood fantasy life consisted of three main elements or themes:

1. The dream of soft, comfy living like a Roman emperor, with my every whim quickly satisfied.

2. Prince Charming, riding in on a white steed from Disneyland with Cinderella to rescue me from the terrors of life—poverty, illness, anti-Semitism, boredom, etc.

3. A philanthropist of immense wealth. (Herein was my secret persona, my true Undiscovered Self—the Count of Monte Cristo, the superrich, hidden hero.) Even more intoxicating than my brother's vast collections of cowboy and Indian tin soldiers and BB guns was the Count's great fat wads of "funny money," Confederate dollars, and Monopoly game "dough," an endless supply of riches! I loved to carry a big roll of pretty, colored, but worthless "Big Bucks" in my pocket to show how important and great I was, someone no cruel Scrooge welfare case worker dared to mess with!

Herein lies the source of my magical relation to money and reality, the desperate need of a lonely, sensitive, victimized child to extricate himself from an overwhelming dilemma—powerlessness over poverty. I created a phony abundance as a cocoon of safety and never really grew up to establish a mature, adult relation to money and wealth. "When you're rich, they can't touch you or push you around." Even my parents bought this idea of money as a shield from life. Their favorite expression was, "Hey, they're filthy with money," that is, objects of awe and respect.

I chose to become a social worker in Public Assistance to work out the demon of impotence, and because my mother was in awe of such powerful positions as Welfare Supervisor, as we had suffered at their hands in closing our cases arbitrarily. I became a supervisor to make Mama proud and to hopefully prevent future abuses against others.

But, oh, the Count of Monte Cristo! Even now the center of my living room has a small shrine surrounded by two boxes of treasure and jewels. On my junkets to Las Vegas and Atlantic City, how I loved the clickety-clack sound of ivory-plastic markers thrown on the roulette table to the call, "Place your bets!" Oh, "Faites vos jeux" in Casablanca—Rick's Club! Oh, glamour! Oh, Hollywood! Oh, escapism! For a night I was not Saul, but James Bond with $10,000 markers. How sophisticated, how debonair, how chic!

How broke!

Now, the creation of credit cards was to me a fabulous event equal in wonder to Orville Wright's flying machine. Funny money was transformed into "crazy credit," funds on demand. You put your plastic card in a box, and out came a fur coat at Bloomingdale's, without cash. Unfortunately, a month later a bill came to my home requesting immediate payment—that's not like Snow White in Disneyland! I was offended and dismayed by the tone of demand and threat of these letters and calls from collection agencies to my Imperial James Bond, Count of Monte Cristo. Alas, there was no Prince Charming to rescue me and demolish my debts.

I found my true salvation in an Overeaters Anonymous meeting. In 1981, I came to Debtors Anonymous and listened, an unemployed social worker deeply in debt, owing $5,500 to creditors. All I had to show for being a Count was a drawer full of tissue-paper slips marked Visa, MasterCard, and Northeast Bank.

My first D.A. sponsor, Jane S., immediately taught me how to deal with nasty collection agencies and pushy creditors. However, my first pressure group with Bill L. and Rhoda F. was a scene of cold-turkey withdrawal out of *Man with the Golden Arm*, *The Lost Weekend*, or *Days of Wine and Roses*. I sweated like a pig! I got a spending plan, an action plan, and a debt repayment plan that changed my life. I found in the Twelve Steps a gift from my HP, a way up and out, a gift of clarity sweeping the fog and mist of delusion away, revealing a beautiful, shining city on a hill.

Now I live one day at a time, trusting that it's OK to live this life in the real world rather than in my head. I've found that reality can be a good friend, not a bleak, empty wasteland; that Disney tales can be cruel, but most important of all, that my HP (Hope Perpetual) is always there for me, my Prince on a white steed, and that the truly abundant life is not one of imperial, aristocratic, glamorous rescuer illusions and fantasies, but a life of service, love, honesty, and purity, which the Promises offer.

I guess I'm finally OK, and it's great!

Originally published in the 2008 second-quarter issue of *Ways & Means* as "A Perpetual Dreamer Finally Faces Reality."

36

D.A. Recovery: Take Two

A debtor drives to the edge before turning back to D.A.

I came to Debtors Anonymous for the first time when I had six years of re-covery in Alcoholics Anonymous, A.C.A., and Al-Anon. I was a divorced single mom of a seven-year-old boy and a full-time student at the local uni-versity. We were living on student loans, welfare, and my part-time income. It was late summer, and we had just moved into a beautiful, roomy apartment, with a good friend as a roommate. Soon after that, I clearly heard little voices telling me it was all very nice, and we could lose it by Christmas. I talked about my fears of self-sabotage in A.A. meetings, and several people who were also in Debtors Anonymous started talking to me about D.A.

I began to attend meetings and knew this was the place for me, but I hated it. My experience with A.A. had been just the opposite. I had felt I was com-ing home and had found the first safe place in the world, maintaining sobriety from the first day I attended.

I began working with a Pressure Relief Group. Both people had over three years in D.A., old-timers in our area. I tried to do everything they suggested. My A.A. sponsor never had trouble with money, so I decided it would be all right to work my Steps around money issues with her. After all, she obviously had it together. She didn't disagree! I avoided the people I knew from my other program in D.A. meetings because I was "too embarrassed" to talk to them.

With the help of my Pressure Relief Group, I learned to keep records. I closed my checking account and used only cash because writing checks had no sense of reality for me. One day at a time I didn't incur new debt. I opened months of bills and notices from creditors. I organized everything in a notebook. My phone was cut off, and I borrowed from my boyfriend to have it turned back on. I hadn't ever told him how bad things were financially. He just knew things were tight because I was a student and a mom. I had never borrowed money from him in the three years we had dated, and I was ashamed to take money from him. I blamed my phone being cut off on my Pressure Relief Group.

Christmas came, and I had the most amazing holiday. I had virtually no money, and my Pressure Relief Group had me meditate each day on what my Higher Power would have me write down as gifts for people on my list. My son ended up receiving everything on the list from other people, and I wasn't able to buy him one of those things. It was a humbling lesson for me about not being the Source.

Another surprise was a marriage proposal from my boyfriend. I was very happy when I came to my next Pressure Relief Group with the news. They were supportive and helped me prepare to tell him about my financial history. I wanted him to see it all before we got married. We started to work on my spending plan. They also suggested my fiancé come to a Pressure Relief Group, so we could plan our non-debting wedding together. That was my last meeting with them.

Two and a half years later, I was sitting on a curb outside an A.A. meeting sobbing about how suicidal I was feeling. The friend I was talking to patted me on the back and said, "I think you need to go back to D.A. I think you missed something important the first time."

I came back to D.A. convinced I was going to die. During my two-year debting spree, I had been employed in the profession I had studied for and made good money. But we were thousands of dollars deeper in debt than when we had married. We had credit cards. We lived from cut-off notice to cut-off notice. We were behind in our rent. And then, I lost my job. The balls we were frantically juggling all dropped and went careening wildly in all directions. I couldn't breathe. I couldn't eat. I couldn't find a job. I was immobilized most of the time.

I approached D.A. differently this time around. I immediately made a service commitment. I found a D.A. sponsor and began working the Steps. I went to every meeting I could. I called people. My daily terror increased dramatically as I made the commitment not to debt, one day at a time. The first woman I asked to sit on my Pressure Relief Group said she would, but she needed me to know she had filed bankruptcy in D.A.; it had been the correct thing for her. I couldn't have cared less about why she thought it was important for me to know that. I just needed to do everything suggested so I wouldn't die!

Powerlessness and unmanageability were not difficult to admit. I felt completely abandoned by my Higher Power, so walking through Steps Two and Three was arduous. The morning I was finally able to make the decision to turn my will and my life over, I prayed in front of the little altar in our bedroom. I acknowledged the desire to know my Higher Power and committed to working the rest of the Steps to complete my spiritual awakening. I humbly prayed, "I know you are the Source. Please, show me how to accept what you have to give. Show me how I can best be of service to my world. I know I am a channel, not the Source." There was a lightening of my entire being. A couple of minutes later I was headed downstairs when my husband walked in the front door with the news, "Honey, I quit my job." My first reaction was, "He isn't the Source either." I had a day of complete peace. My terror returned the next day, but I had done my Third Step and nothing could remove the impact of that decision.

By the time I had completed my inventory and was trying to share it with my sponsor, it was clear I could no longer work with her. I was grateful for the time we had spent. She had clarified so much about what brought me to D.A. I wasn't finding anyone else I wanted to work with, and sitting on my completed Fourth Step was making me nuttier than I already was. There wasn't much room for decline! After having her name come to me several times while praying for help, I did my Fifth Step with a program friend who is a therapist. She is well acquainted with D.A. and incest recovery. She also helped me with my list of outdated survival skills that were surfacing at the beginning of my Step Six.

A week or so later, I was in the town eight miles north of where I lived. I knew I would drive off the freeway and kill myself if I tried to go home. I was able to get to the local mental institution. They invited me to stay, but I refused. They treated me for anxiety and depression, and I went home. I began to work with a therapist on my chronic depression and anxiety. I had lived with them all my life and didn't know. I took medication for eight months to help relieve the symptoms. It enabled me to finally dive into the deepest core of my experience, feelings I had not been able to touch in my nine years of Step work and therapy.

About a month after my close call with suicide, I had the opportunity to attend the D.A. World Conference. My husband went with me, hoping to hear something that would help him, but he didn't think he had anything in common with anyone there. I absorbed the entire day. My soul stirred when I heard one woman speak on the Visions panel. Next week I tracked her down and asked her to be my sponsor. She lived forty miles away, but I was willing to go anywhere to work with her. She asked for time to pray about it and called a few days later, agreeing to sponsor me. Then we met for the first time. Our long-distance relationship has worked well, and we have continued even though she now lives in another state.

I spent my first two years in almost daily terror. Things looked worse financially. We went deeper into debt. Work was sporadic and unpredictable for both of us. My compulsions got much worse, and I injured myself at work. Our home was not a pleasant place most of the time.

By continuing to work the Steps, work with my sponsor and my Pressure Relief Group, go to meetings, talk to people, and make friends in D.A., I have learned to see how my basic needs are being met each day. When I project ahead one bit, I fret and worry, and sometimes quickly, sometimes slowly, end up in terror again. I know I don't need to act on anything when I am feeling urgency.

I have had a very difficult time with my faith. It finally occurred to me a few months ago that I didn't see or feel the same about anything anymore, but I was waiting to have the same comfortable feelings about my Higher Power that I had in my first years of recovery. Since that day, I have just prayed to please be shown what I need to see and to feel what I need to feel. I didn't know how it should be. The wonderful woman who sat on my Pressure Relief Group for over two years constantly urged me to go inside to learn what was correct for me. My sponsor told me it is my responsibility to check within before making decisions. Now I have learned how to identify some of my needs, accept them, and act on getting them met.

Both people who now sit on my Pressure Relief Group are able to accept abundance in most areas of their lives. I want to believe I deserve abundance, too. My husband started attending D.A. nine months ago, and we have been current on all bills for five months. We have a goal to begin debt repayment this year. Our home is loving and supportive, and our family flourishes. We started a D.A. Couples Meeting in our home. I am still disabled from my work injury, but my sponsor keeps reminding me this is a gift of time. I recognize that at times, and I am grateful. I am taking art classes for the first time in my life and exploring new career opportunities.

Maybe it is because I am a recovering alcoholic/addict, but I was not able to fully commit to D.A. recovery until my behavior became life-threatening. On the days I don't want to keep going, I have the day I couldn't get on the freeway to look back on. I know I can only go forward or I will die, so I keep taking each small step. I am learning I don't have to do things alone. D.A. is teaching me to find and accept all kinds of support. I try to treat myself in a loving way each minute of every day. And I try to treat all others the same way. I am so thankful for the Steps, Tools, and people of D.A. They have saved me and given me a rich life.

Originally published in the first edition of *A Currency of Hope*.

37

No Longer a Thief

This woman stopped taking from others after learning how to give to herself.

Why was the police car in front of our house? Had something happened to Mom or Dad? I entered the house through the garage door; the front door was for holidays or guests.

Sitting around our kitchen table were my Mom and Dad, along with two police officers. I was told to sit at the table, this same table where I ate with the family, or played Scrabble, or poured drinks for Mom and Dad. Today the faces were all serious and angry—even disgusted. On the kitchen table were black-and-white drawings with the word "suspect" and the description: White female, five-foot-five, one hundred twenty pounds, blonde, approximate age, twelve to fifteen years.

I was quiet that day. I listened intently as my parents explained why stealing is bad and wrong—even dangerous. My parents said they were ashamed of me, so disappointed. I looked in my Mom's eyes and saw hatred. I already thought she was jealous of me. More than once in her drunkenness, she had told me I was not pretty or smart. Often she said I would not get so much attention if people knew who I really was. And that day I knew she was right. I was so terrified that I never stole anything from that store again.

But a few months went by and I needed makeup. I used a lot of makeup, but had trouble choosing the right kind. I couldn't afford to make a mistake, so I just took it. If it was not perfect, it wouldn't hurt. I knew that if I could just have the right makeup, I would be good, beautiful, and lovable.

When I was younger, I had enjoyed frequent walks to the neighborhood Quick-Stop with my friends for candy or a popsicle, some very sweet treat. During those walks, I would reluctantly reveal that I had only a small amount of change, so my friends would pool their money to get me a treat, too. I must be lovable, I would think; friends buy me treats. My parents praised me to their friends for being careful with money. My sister, on the other hand, could not hold onto money: "Money burns a hole in that girl's pocket," my dad would often say.

At Christmas there were many sweets, presents, cards, visitors, calls, and festivities, but it was too much at once and only once a year. The time it took to unwrap everything was awesome! I would open one present after another, but it seemed as though I was looking for something that was never there. There was too much pressure to be surprised and happy about the gifts, and I knew I could never be grateful enough. I was embarrassed. I didn't let anyone know I felt this way, of course. I would be in a store soon, and there I would see something that would make the difference. I would take it; then I would be satisfied.

As I grew up, I became a sophisticated thief. I stole from friends and family, department stores, and small businesses. I was out of control. I had gotten everything I demanded, and still I felt empty. Perhaps more would make a difference the next time.

By the age of thirty, I had been married to the man of my childhood dreams for ten years. We had our second brand-new home in the suburbs, a nice new car in the two-car garage, and a new BMW touring motorcycle. We had a beautiful, healthy one-and-a-half-year-old son. Our family was complete now, yet I was miserable. I felt bad and ugly. I felt love only for my son and believed I had become completely unlovable. It took a little more than two years to lose everything but the responsibility of caring for my son.

I had been clean and sober four years and had cleaned up much "wreckage from the past," as they say in A.A. Around the Fellowship, I was known as a woman who took her sobriety seriously. I worked the Steps. I read and loved the "Big Book" of Alcoholics Anonymous. I kept regular contact with my sponsor and my sponsees. I was even in therapy. I was truly committed to doing my emotional work and my family-of-origin inventory. I wanted to be free, yet I was afraid most of the time. And no matter how hard I worked and budgeted, I never had enough money to get through the month.

I took in boarders, though I hated people living in the house with me and my son to meet expenses. I used my two credit cards at the end of every month for a treat for us, or gifts for someone. I would try to do without all month; then I would need relief. Credit cards or stealing seemed the only way. I didn't plan to steal; it was usually an afterthought. I knew something was very wrong that I felt so bad and was still stealing. I was particularly vulnerable at the cosmetic counter. I was willing to pay for mascara, but not the two lip liners. What was happening to me? I had never been caught stealing. My only close call was that day long ago in the kitchen with the police officers.

Early one fall, I was out with a friend. In the middle of my whining about money problems, my friend said she was not at all sure my problem was debting or compulsive spending. She did tell me that she had been going to a program called Debtors Anonymous and that this program was helping her to live free of worry about money. I trusted this friend and, on that alone, I went to my first D.A. meeting. I hated being new. I hated being there at all. It felt so shameful! I did not even understand the word "debting," although I did feel some understanding of compulsive spending. I was sure my problem was that I wanted too much: I needed help to control my spending so I could have enough money to pay all my bills every month, including those awful credit card balances that continued to grow in spite of my paying the minimum every month. I couldn't see how to do it without credit cards.

I did cut up my credit cards during the first month of going to D.A. meetings. I was terrified. I suffered from sleeplessness, panic attacks, and rage. I used my small prudent reserve in a few months trying to do it all without credit cards or boarders. I would pay all my bills, including credit card debts and my student loans. Then I would see there was not enough money left for us to live on for the rest of the month. I tried to juggle the amount I spent on food or gas, and I cut out all entertainment for me or my son. The deprivation would make me crazy each month. My life was getting worse: It was harder, and now I began to bounce checks at the end of the month.

Out of desperation, I finally began to talk in meetings, sharing my confusion, anger, and terror. I began to have Pressure Relief Groups, and after about nine months, surrendered to the truth that I really could not meet my needs and continue to make debt repayment. I was horrified at the thought of inviting bill collectors into my already terrifying life, but I saw I had no choice. I had seen others in the Fellowship learn to place their own needs first, and their lives were changing. They were less worried. These people were talking about taking vacations and having fun. I wanted to stop stealing. I, too, wanted to be free.

I worked hard at my D.A. recovery. I loved and used all the tools available to me. I attended meetings and talked to people on the phone, sometimes bookending a shopping trip. I even made phone calls from stores when I felt that dizzy confusion. I prayed a lot to my God for direction and guidance. This new way of living required such focus. I fielded the phone calls from bill collectors. I cried and screamed my way through the shame and the humiliation. I finally began to separate myself from what I earn, own, or owe, but I was still overwhelmed by the feeling that there was really not enough for me in the world. Whenever I did begin to believe there might be enough, I would shrink with the feeling that I was not enough. Then I would steal and hate myself even more. I dared to talk about stealing in meetings. I had felt so alone with my shame.

After a year and a half in D.A., my world filled with death and grief. Within a summer, twelve people I knew and cared about died or were murdered. I hurt, crying for weeks. I rarely left my house, only occasionally going to my favorite meetings where I would just sit and cry. Sometimes I shared and people just listened. Thank God no one tried to fix me or asked me to leave. One afternoon, I came back from a meeting feeling quiet, not so sad. I went to a store to buy a few things I needed, and I saw a large assortment of flowers outside the store. I took two plants and put them in the back of my car. I drove home and carefully hung my beautiful new plants from the deck. For weeks, I spent most of my daylight hours sitting on the deck either crying, reading fairy tales, or staring quietly into space. I needed the flowers for hope and for their beauty.

I sat on the deck and looked at my flowers and suddenly understood, for the first time in my life, that I stole because I believed there was not enough in this world for me and that I did not deserve anything good or beautiful. I believed that I was bad, ugly, even rotten to the core, as I had heard my mother say so often when I was a little girl. I believed I was unlovable. In that moment, I understood that every time I stole, I was reinforcing those beliefs I had picked up in my childhood. I cried and through my tears, I asked God to be interested in me, my life, and to help me to believe that I was good, beautiful, and lovable. I needed to open myself up to the generosity of God.

There were many more months of tears that year, but I never felt alone again. I never stole anything, even when I had intense feelings of lack or deprivation. Now I was on different footing. I was learning to care for myself and be the grown-up in my own life.

Five more years have passed since then. I stay close to D.A. I truly love my group and have stayed in service to my Monday night meeting. I continue to use the Tools of the program, and I love the action plans that are generated from my Pressure Relief Groups. My action steps now consist of shopping for new furniture and saving for a trip to Europe with my teenage son. I receive loving encouragement to be gentle and loving to myself. I am supported by D.A. to give myself love, comfort, even luxury. I have come a long way on this journey. Stealing is something I used to do. Now I can trust myself and my God to love and take care of me.

In a Visions meeting in my second year of recovery in D.A., I saw myself holding hands with a partner. I had a feeling of love, warmth, and comfort. Today I have that partnership with myself. I am no longer consumed by the isolation or the tragic loneliness that a compulsive, addicted person knows. My family is in my life again. What a miracle! Now I love and care about them just the way they are. Today, the greatest gifts from my recovery work are the relationships I have with myself and others. It has happened: I am good, beautiful, and lovable! Thanks D.A.! And thank God for the Twelve Steps.

Originally published in the first edition of *A Currency of Hope*.

38

The Answer to a Family Disease

*She blamed others until she learned to accept her
own powerlessness over compulsive debting.*

"... acceptance is the answer to *all* my problems. ..."
—The "Big Book" of Alcoholics Anonymous

I did not have a problem with money. My late husband had a problem with money. He would overspend compulsively and then try to cut back all at once. I never had the problems he did, but when he asked me to cut back, I would go out and buy something. But I did not have a problem with money.

After my husband died, I cut up about fifteen credit cards of his. I only kept four or five "just in case!" I was determined not to lose control over my money, but whenever I worked on paying bills and figuring out my finances, I would get so confused and be in so much pain that I would walk away from my desk saying (in my best Scarlett O'Hara imitation), "I'll think about it in the morning—tomorrow is another day."

But I did not have a problem with money. My daughter had a problem with money. She could never account for where her money went or how to save. Then she joined this group called Debtors Anonymous and miracles happened over and over in her life. Visions of moving, of right work, of going back to school—all were realized. She is the person who attracted me into D.A. She remains one of my life coaches.

When I looked at my daughter's miracles, my denial broke. I realized that blaming my late husband got to be a pretty thin excuse after twelve years of widowhood! I got busy and applied the Tools—keeping my numbers, going to meetings, using the phone, becoming aware of the power of credit advertising, and of course having Pressure Relief Meetings. My PRG lady became my sponsor, and a role model for me.

I was never in much debt—not even $1,000. But debt is debt, and guilt and shame were my companions. Gradually I began to voice my visions for retirement, for a smaller place to live, and for travel. Thanks to D.A. I was able to retire three years earlier than I originally planned. I found a condo that suits my lifestyle perfectly. I have traveled extensively at home and abroad. I was able to manage my late mother's finances with ease and integrity for the last five years of her life.

I have been in debt-free recovery for sixteen years. Thanks to D.A. and its Steps and Traditions I have been able to receive the love and guidance of my D.A. peers, to sponsor and be sponsored, and to give service at the group, Intergroup, and World Service levels. I have learned when and how to say "No" when it is time for rotation of service. I dedicate a specific amount of money in my spending plan to distribute at meetings and also to go directly to the D.A. GSB every month.

Thank you, D.A., for fulfilling all of the Promises in my life and bringing me joy and serenity.

Originally posted on the Debtors Anonymous website as "D.A. Recovery Is the Answer to a Family Disease."

How to Find
Debtors Anonymous

At the time of this printing, there are more than 500 listed meetings of Debtors Anonymous in almost all fifty of the United States. Known meetings also exist on six continents: North America, South America, Europe, Asia, Africa, and Australia.

The Debtors Anonymous General Service Board, Inc., maintains an office through which one can obtain additional information about D.A. worldwide. Please write to the following address for information:

D.A. General Service Office
P.O. Box 920888
Needham, MA 02492-0009
(781) 453-2743
(800) 421-2383 (U.S.A. only)

In many larger metropolitan areas in the United States, one may find a listing for a local Debtors Anonymous telephone number in the local telephone directory. Local social service agencies that make referrals to Twelve-Step programs may also have information about Debtors Anonymous in their areas. Other traditional sources for locating Twelve-Step meetings, such as newspapers, clergy, community service centers, and referral services, also may help you find D.A. meetings in your area.

Debtors Anonymous has a website on the World Wide Web:

www.debtorsanonymous.org

Information available through this website includes meeting listings, general facts about D.A., questions to ask yourself to help determine if D.A. may be appropriate for you, information for the media, information to access registered online groups, literature order forms, and current news for members.

Business Debtors Anonymous (B.D.A.) gives information specific to business owners and self-employed professionals. B.D.A. is fully embraced by Debtors Anonymous, but it has distinct concerns of special interest to its members.

Notes

Made in United States
North Haven, CT
30 October 2024

59659172R00117